# THE HERO'S JOURNEY

*A COURSE ON SELF-ESTEEM*

Meditations on

Addiction

Recovery

and

Transformation

by

Gary W. Reece, Ph.D.

Resource *Publications*
An imprint of *Wipf and Stock Publishers*
150 West Broadway • Eugene OR 97401

Resource *Publications*
an imprint of Wipf and Stock Publishers
150 West Broadway
Eugene, Oregon 97401

The Hero's Journey
A Course on Self-Esteem
By Reece, Gary W.
©1997 Reece, Gary W.
ISBN: 1-57910-639-0
Publication date: April, 2001
Previously published by The Stepcare Institute, 1997.

# DEDICATION

This project has come about through the inspiration, support, encouragement, and opportunity provided by numerous people. Susan Laufer-Casorla, Publisher of L.A. Steps for Recovery, originally suggested the articles on Self-esteem and graciously published them. Dr. John Sims of the Prevailing Word Ministry took on the Herculean task of teaching me how to operate a computer and has consistently and patiently provided the technical and tutorial assistance I have needed to complete this project. I would also like to thank my clients whose stories provide the foundation and inspiration for my meditations. Greg Wheeler, Ph.D., a friend and colleague has put in hundreds of hours in helping me get my Web Page up and running. I deeply appreciate his dedication to my project and the encouragement he has given me by his belief in the value of my contributions. Finally, it has been a source of continuous joy to have my son, Brandon Scott Reece, involved. His photographic genius is responsible for the cover and the back photograph. Thank you all.

Gary W. Reece, Ph.D.
Sierra Madre
California            November 1997

# TABLE OF CONTENTS

| | | | |
|---|---|---|---|
| Introduction | | | 1 |
| Chapter | 1 | Inner Healing | 5 |
| Chapter | 2 | Self-esteem | 27 |
| Chapter | 3 | Addiction | 45 |
| Chapter | 4 | Relationships | 65 |
| Chapter | 5 | Anger | 87 |
| Chapter | 6 | Depression | 109 |
| Chapter | 7 | Shame and Guilt | 129 |
| Chapter | 8 | Identity | 155 |
| Chapter | 9 | Recovery | 177 |
| Chapter | 10 | Fear | 201 |
| Chapter | 11 | Love | 223 |
| Chapter | 12 | Spirituality | 247 |

# Prologue

## Dunes

shadowy,    shifting,      undulating moonlit
   mounds
sharp edged   soft contours   fluid particles in
concert
       silent symphony of elements

I entered alien    separate   the knower and
definer     EGO        footsteps     blurring
   disappearing      am     not     am     not
i am no more

presence      silence     solitude    full moon
rising      collision      earth and sky
       boundary blurring         transformation
stillness         at one ment   knower and known
fluid   whole     all of one piece    the great
tapestry     divesting    shifting boundaries
melding into the all

dunes     the eternal metaphor      process
unfolding      going along for the ride
       substance      essence     transformation
a mysterious transcendent moment

a light show in sand
                    eternity incarnate


           Death Valley

   Sand Dunes       1-20-92


written after sitting in silence for several
hours as the moon rose over the dunes   gr

# INTRODUCTION

*One thing that comes out in myths is that at the bottom of the abyss comes the voice of salvation. The black moment is the moment when the real message of transformation is going to come. At the darkest moment comes the light. Joseph Campbell*

One of the great mysteries in life is that of death and rebirth which is symbolized in all of the great myths and stories passed on from ancient to modern civilization. In these stories as examined by Joseph Campbell, the great mythologist of our age, the universal insight is that spiritual transformation comes when we enter that dark night of the soul symbolized by the wasteland or the abyss. Those who suffer from problems with addiction know this reality as hitting bottom.

As far back as I can remember I have been interested in how people change and how they can be helped in the process. Because of a series of events in my own life, I have also been very concerned with transformation. Out of necessity I have sought answers to the deepest questions posed by my own darkness, despair and isolation. In search of answers I turned inward for understanding and greater awareness. This writing project has evolved from that quest. Three years ago I began writing a series of monthly articles on self-esteem for L.A. Steps for Recovery. As I struggled each month to find a topic, I noticed that I was using my own experience and that of my clients as sources of inspiration and illumination. Also during this process I discovered I began changing as I meditated on these topics.

I discovered, that out of this continual struggle to find answers I was not only gaining knowledge, but inner healing was taking place. I thought I might be on to something, so I kept exploring and this volume of essays is the result. I found that meditating on a theme raised my level of awareness and brought that particular issue to the foreground of my consciousness. As this happened I found myself living with greater awareness. As I struggled with my inner demons I was also effecting the long sought for acceptance, forgiveness, and serenity. I discovered a simple formula for transformation:

**Awareness + Analysis + Action = Transformation.**

In this essay I am concerned with the big issue of transformation as it works itself out in the arena of addiction and recovery. The window through which I view this process is that of self-esteem. This perspective stems from the awareness I gained on my own recovery journey: that, at the heart of self-destructiveness is injured self-esteem.

The structure of this work is organized around the topic of self-esteem and all of the various related issues. For the reader to achieve maximum benefit I have organized my meditations into topics. I recommend that you first read the introduction to each topic which will establish a basic framework and some common concepts; once this is done, then I recommend that you spend time meditating on the theme, then do some writing and inner exploration around the topic. Live with it for a while and then notice any new awareness which might generate insight into needed areas of transformation. Then think about how you might want to change. The next step is to visualize yourself being different. Finally, develop a target for change and then work out a plan of action. The book is designed to teach each individual how to discover their inner sense of worth and significance by using guided imagery, journaling, intensive self-exploration, relaxation, meditation, and visualization. I have created a four stage experiential approach which looks like this:

**1. RECOGNIZE:** In this stage the attitudes, thoughts, ideas and self-talk (cognitive domain) are explored along with strategies for changing long held and deeply ingrained habits of thought, self-talk, attitudes and expectations.

**2. ANALYZE:** Examine the material you have brought to conscious awareness. Notice patterns, and recurring themes. Do not ask why, but rather; how. How does this work, what happens when I do this? Look for triggers. Look for the payoff. What purpose does this behavior serve? Under what conditions did I learn how to do this? Does it still work? What rewards maintain this behavior? What would I lose if I changed this habit? This is the essence of behavioral analysis.

**3. VISUALIZE:** Guided Imagery, relaxation, meditation, and visualization are used to intensify the transformation process. each person is encouraged to take the journey of self-exploration to reconnect with resources of power and vitality which empower the actualization of self-esteem.

**4. ACTUALIZE:** Strategies for integrating feelings, imagery, awareness, thoughts, and behaviors for consciously transforming self-esteem are taught so that each individual may become the architect and creator of their emerging self.

Meister Eckhart, a 13th century Dominican mystic put self-transformation in this framework: "Our spiritual journey is waking up to the divine sea in which we swim."

This awakening comes as we embrace mystery, seek the self in solitude, listen in silence for the inner voice of awareness to speak of our journey, and surrender to the awesome call of the nobility and royalty of being a self.

In this process we give birth to a new self, an authentic, compassionate, loving, aware, self. It requires diligence, and the patience to surf the infinity horizons of awareness: an awakened consciousness.

## *Bon Voyage!*

\* To facilitate this journey, I have created three audio tapes to teach you 1) Relaxation, 2) Meditation, and 3) Self-affirmation. See the order blank at the back of the book.

# 1

# INNER HEALING

What is this thing called inner healing? The terms wounded and healing are bandied about with such great glibness these days, we act as if we know what we mean when we use these terms. My hunch is that everyone has their own private understanding and definition of these words. This is my own private philosophy; truth and meaning are always personal and they come out of our own particular personal histories. The problem for most people is that they do not understand this simple principle: *truth is subjective.* We get into trouble when we "expect" others to act on the basis of our truth. They in fact are acting on their truth. We always assume our "truth" to be valid and universal. It is not! We do have shared truth, but even then it is always filtered through my experience and yours. Sometimes we meet and even understand each other, or at least think we do. It is important in particular to understand this simple idea when it comes to talking about wounding and healing. I have a whole host of presumptions and biases which need to be taken into consideration when I write about this process. In fact that is precisely the point. We always come to the table with our biases. We will have a greater chance of understanding each other if we accept, know and own our biases. Having said all of that, let me proceed with sharing how I have come to look at this wondrous thing (process) called healing. I assume the reader is aware that millions of pages have been written on this topic and that I will have to be very brief in my discussion. This is the frustrated college teacher in me, always wanting to define my terms and provide extensive background without leaving out anything important.

Our view of wounding depends on our paradigm. In psychology there are several paradigms: behavioral (learning), physiological (disease) humanistic (social and psychological) and transpersonal (deistic or theistic). All of these influence our view of what is wrong with us and how we go about fixing it. Paul Tillich, my favorite theologian, once wrote, there are three questions of importance, (1) What does it mean to be whole? (2) What is wrong with us? and (3) How shall we be restored? I think that this just about covers it. Inner healing, wounding and recovery are very personal answers to these questions as they are encountered in the problems of living.

I take the position that we are spiritual beings who bear the image of our creator. Living is the struggle to actualize this image. Therefore being wounded and healing are spiritual problems. They arise out of our being in the world. Though we bear the marks of our heritage and are capable of consciousness of immortality, we are mortal. That is our problem, mortals who would be gods. There is no solution to our dilemma. We die, but we live as if we are going to live forever. Death, loneliness, meaningless, isolation, freedom, guilt and responsibility; these are the fundamental problems of being human. This is our condition. St. Augustine once wrote, "It is only in the face of death that man's self is born." With the risk of trying to improve on St. Augustine, I would paraphrase him by saying that it is only as we confront the problems of existence that our self is born. The implications for this are very important. This makes the self, *intentional, conscious, free, and capable of transformation.*

Let us start with the most fundamental concept which is necessary for building a foundation for healing. Healing cannot take place unless one thing occurs. I must take responsibility for my life. Responsibility means authorship! To be aware of responsibility is to be aware of creating one's own self, destiny, life predicament, feelings, and if such be the case, one's own suffering. For if we do not accept such responsibility, and persist in blaming others, or `life' for our predicament, no real change is possible! The beginning of illumination or enlightenment only comes when we see through the veil of our defenses and "get it". I am responsible, I am the creator of my life in all of its complexity, paradox, and vexation. It is in this sense that we give birth to ourselves daily by the choices we make. This is what is meant by *actualizing the imago.*

A second and necessary fundamental of healing is that my whole life is the issue. My very "mode of being in the world" is what I have constructed as my personal answer to the riddle of my existence. It is designed to answer the "who am I?" question. I also need to answer other fundamental questions such as the meaning of my life and my death, as well as who others are to me, the nature of the universe, and how I can live in a fulfilling way. And finally, how I balance my desires with the responsibilities I have to my family and my community. In short, what must I do to be saved? These are the great theological-spiritual-philosophical questions which have confronted mankind since the first humans sat around a fire and began to talk to each other, tell stories, and paint their experiences on the walls of their caves.

A third fundamental idea is that our "pathology", or that which is wrong with us is "symptomatic" of our mode of being in the world. In simpler terms, our way of living generates consequences. Our bodies, and emotions will tell us about the success of our journey. In other words, when we get `symptomatic' the symptoms tell us that our hero journey is developing problems. Anxiety, depression, guilt, and loneliness are all natural byproducts of living. We cannot live without being wounded. It is *how* we we respond to our being wounded which is at issue. Again, if we are responsible for our life (self) project and ultimately our predicament, then we are also ultimately responsible for our healing.

How, then, do we heal ourselves? "It is only as we confront the problems of existence that our self is born." It is in this mystery that both wounding and healing are taking place simultaneously. We live and are wounded, and so we need to heal the wounds that come from our unique situations. This is the first point of wisdom. My wounds are uniquely my own.

Responsibility for myself subtly shifts my perceptions from being a helpless victim in the world to a self-responsible creator of my own destiny. This is the beginning of empowerment and enlightenment. I cannot emphasize enough the importance of this principle. It is the pivot point for the journey. The second important point of wisdom is **Awareness**. In many respects, this is the point of the journey. So many of the great religions have this as their foundation: "heightened awareness, enlightenment as the ultimate state of being, to be the enlightened one is the purpose of the journey. Awareness is both a precondition for growth as well as the outcome. Awareness creates a shifting of our perceptions and leads to expanding the horizons of our consciousness, therefore we live less unconsciously. When we live unconsciously we are living blindly. We are ruled by our impulses, we act out our conflicts, and our emotions rule the day. The goal of psychoanalysis according to Freud was to "make the unconscious conscious".

There are many ways to accomplish this, a prolonged course of psychoanalysis is only one way. There are many others: some formal and others informal. In this essay I am advocating a highly personal inner journey as a way of accomplishing the goal of enlightened living. This course on Self-esteem is designed to take you deeply into your inner being in a way which leads to greater awareness and wholeness. The method I advocate is called **Dialectics**.

Dialectics is a method of inquiry which I have borrowed from philosophy. I use it as a means of creating awareness by working with paradox, conflict and mystery. We do this by giving ourselves up to the process and learning to live in the polarities of life. The Zen Masters use basically the same techniques. They ask their students to ponder a mystery which is a **Koan**. Meditating on a riddle causes the student to increase his awareness and by trying to reconcile seemingly impossible polarities leaps onto a whole new plane of perception. The paradigm shifts and enlightenment occurs. How does this work in psychological terms?

Dialectics requires several things. The first is an

attitude. You must be committed to self-discovery. You must desire wholeness. In other words, you must become a pilgrim and make discovery your highest value. Seek and you will find, knock and it will be opened to you. You must make your recovery the highest priority in your life. When you do this you have placed a high value on your spiritual well-being. In this case it is a question of values and priorities. As Jesus once said, "where a man's heart is there shall be his treasure also." He asked the question, "What shall it profit a man if he gain the whole world, but lose his soul?" Values prioritize our goals and striving. Tillich puts it in this light, whatever is your ultimate concern, that is your God. The danger is in worshiping things which are not worthy of our devotion. As Nietzsche once said, **"Hold fast to the Hero in you soul, hold sacred your highest hope."** This is the kind of commitment I am talking about.

Dialectics requires focused attention, solitude and silence. All of the great mystical traditions emphasize silence and meditation as a means of gaining inner peace and awareness. In order to get to know yourself you must spend quality time with you. Do this by spending some time each day in quiet meditation where you pay attention to what is going on inside you. Sit quietly and let yourself become aware. Pay attention to your feelings, thoughts, and fleeting images which may pass through your consciousness. Listen to your inner dialogue and pay attention to your inner newsreel. Do not judge or censor anything. Keep a trip log, write down what you are experiencing. The most important thing is to let yourself feel your feelings. This is called centering. By doing this you are breaking down the defensive barriers which have kept you out of touch with yourself and your feelings. This in itself is a symptom of pathology. Deadness of spirit, disconnected feelings, and consciousness split off from itself is the antithesis of wholeness. This is how we heal: ***feel, interrogate our experiences and reconnect with our history.*** This makes the unconscious conscious and leads to greater awareness. Pay attention to your dreams and fantasies. Freud once said that "Dreams are the royal road to the unconscious." This very exercise I call ***stopping the world.*** Most Americans have a great deal of difficulty in going slowly, listening to themselves, being silent, and being alone.

As material surfaces and we connect with old wounds and the pain of our lives we struggle to make sense of it and to find a way to integrate it into our consciousness. This often causes the next shift of consciousness. A change in our perceptions, ideas, and language. We constitute our experience through language, symbols and myths. These are the ideas we live by, the rules and conventions of our culture. This is how we became a member. These may come into question as we engage in the dialectical process of dealing with the polarities of experience. Synthesis, antithesis and synthesis. This is the dialectical process of experiencing. As we deal with the ambivalence we feel toward someone we allow ourselves to feel the polarities of love and hate, dependence and independence, childlike and adult, anger and tenderness. As we struggle with the ideas, conventions, rules and values we were raised with and try to reconcile them to our present experience we again struggle to create meaning.

Actively engage yourself in disputing your old ideas and

self-talk. Listen for ideas which do not make sense. Listen to what you believe about life. Question your basic assumptions. This is the "story line which has been the continuing theme of your life: your own mytho-poetic journey.

This is part of the process of inner healing; reconciling incongruent, conflicted, absurd, paradoxical, and enigmatic experiences with our need to make sense of experience. According to Joseph Campbell one of the functions of myth is to help us live in accord and harmony with ourselves, our society, and the universe. Working out a personal philosophy is part of the identity struggle. Who am I? What's the purpose of life? How do I come to grips with my own mortality? Why pain, suffering and injustice? What is significant, sacred in my life?

This becomes the next level of the journey, acceptance and forgiveness. As we again and again encounter our personal histories we become faced with material that is often painful and difficult to accept. Guilt, shame, anger, hatred, fear, injuries and self-loathing all are the grist for this part of the journey. Again we wrestle, we struggle with the opposites, conflicts and dissonance. How can we forgive ourselves? How can we forgive others? How can we accept tragedy and chaos? How do we come to grips with the basic stuff of our lives?

Struggling with these problems is what leads to greater awareness, new depths of understanding, a new paradigm, and freedom from old wounds. This is the journey which leads to creation of the self. Our self is born of such strife and struggle.

Out of the depths of our anguish, anxiety and despair we come to appreciate and cherish the gift of life and come to care and have compassion for ourselves. Compassion and care are the healing balm that make the journey possible. They are also the stuff of our relationship with the world. We build ourselves into the world by caring and hold the world together with compassion. These have historically been the markers of great souls. As we struggle with our need to be safe and secure, to have meaning, to feel alive, and to find love, we encounter a world of chaos and absurdity. And as we wrestle with the Identity question and to actualize the image of our creator we struggle with inauthenticity, the need to reduce the world into manageable proportions, with idolatry and the urge to find something, anything, which will give us shelter. In this struggle we realize our vulnerability and fragility, aloneness and mortality. The burden of self-hood and the need to hide our nakedness in the face of an infinite universe: that is the test which gives birth to our self.

**NOTES**

# Meditation
# 1

The journey of inner healing, according to Joseph Campbell, always begins with the wound. In my career as a therapist I have had some remarkable opportunities to work with people in a variety of states of woundedness. This has confirmed for me the truth of Campbell's statement. Have you ever wondered why it takes a crisis to cause us to change? In all of my years of practice, I have never had anyone ever come to see me and say, "I am so abundantly happy that I just want to spend some time growing and learning to deal with my happiness." In fact it is the rule that it is pain which brings people to me and it is pain which sends most people to their physicians. Pain is a signal that something is amiss, it is a symptom of dis-ease. Ordinarily we live our lives on automatic pilot. We go along and do the things we have always done. We live our lives conventionally. We habitually do the things which work, have given us pleasure in the past and which are predictable in their consequences. Why change it if it is working?

On the other hand, habits also work in the same fashion for self-destructive behavior. That is one of the great mysteries of life. Why do people persist in doing things over and over even though it leads to pain and suffering? Habit. The habit was learned and it worked at one time. B.F. Skinner proved this point conclusively when he taught pigeons to peck a lever until they died of starvation. He got them to do this by giving them a food pellet when they pecked a lever. They pecked the lever and got rewarded. The behavior had functional utility--it worked. Then Skinner introduced randomness into the equation, sometimes they didn't get rewarded. So they just increased their lever pecking until they got the reward again. He spaced out the rewards to the point that they were not getting any food. They died trying.

But we are not like pigeons, some would say. Really? Why else would someone put 100 silver dollars into a slot machine without getting one hit? And then turn around and do it again and this time get $10.00. Then, turn around and do it again with no hits. The money is gone and the person can hardly wait to get some money to do it all over. And some call this fun! No wonder suckers are sometimes called "Pigeons." This is the paradigm for addicton.

Though we may be alike, we are also different from pigeons in many respects, and one of the ways is in our response to pain and suffering. Some people after a while pause and engage in conscious, self-reflection. They observe that perhaps what they are doing is not working. And perhaps there might be a better way to live their lives. I have had a number of people express gratitude for a crisis in their lives which served as a wake up call. It caused them to go through a period of intense self-examination and turn their lives around. The pain was the messenger. It told them there was a problem. They examined their lives and discovered the source of the pain. They made changes and began doing things differently. In order to do this they all began with the wound. It was the wound which started them on their inner journey.

My wound occurred in when 1971 my wife and I lost a six-month-old child due to Sudden Infant Death Syndrome. Over the next ten years, I tried to deal with this shattering blow to my world by over-working, over-spending, buying new cars and looking for self-esteem in all the wrong places. Anything which took away the deadness, guilt, failure, depression, terror, rage and confusion, I practiced even when it stopped working. My solutions became problems. They did not restore self-esteem. In fact, they resulted in a vicious cycle of addiction: shame, failure, guilt, compulsion, loss of control and self-hatred. These are he prime drives of addiction. At the core was damaged self-esteem. My inner journey did not begin until 1984 after I had gotten divorced and discovered that I was still unhappy. I realized one day that I was still the same miserable, depressed and lonely individual after the divorce that I was before. Surprise, surprise. And now a few years later I reflect back on the wound and the divorce and feel gratitude that the pain and suffering caused me to take a long look at who I had become so that I could make some needed changes.

**NOTES**

# Meditation 2

The phone call came from a client I had seen a long time ago when he was going though a divorce. Now he was remarried and had two children with his present wife. He was so depressed he could hardly function. His speech was slurred and his thought process was slowed and wandering. He was in deep trouble. He was reaching out again after all these years. I asked him what had happened. "My mother-in-law was diagnosed with cancer, it's terminal." I waited for more. Somehow I had expected an event of greater magnitude to account for the level of dysfunction I was hearing. I do not mean to diminish the significance of his mother-in-law's illness, but I was trying to account for the profound depth of his depression. Usually the magnitude of the loss is in proportion to the suffering. What was going on here? I agreed to see him as soon as he could get to my office.

We began by exploring his feelings about the loss and the news of her illness. Even his wife was shocked at his reaction. "It's my mother, why are you so upset?" Why indeed? He talked some more. He talked of how he had come to love his mother-in-law and how important she had become to him. Roger stopped talking, and a look of consternation came over his face. "I don't know where this is coming from, I'm having this image of my mother lying in bed and I am having to carry out a bucket of blood and vomit. She had stomach cancer and I had to care for her when she was dying. I was 13. I was all alone with her while my father was working." Why indeed? Then he continued, breaking into sobs and said, "now it's a year later and I am in a car at an intersection, my father is slumped over the steering wheel. No one is coming to help me. Two hours go by, finally someone calls my uncle and he comes and we get my father to a hospital. He had a heart attack. Then I had to care for him until he died. I was all alone." Why, Indeed?

Clearly his mother-in-law's situation triggered old traumatic-delayed grief and caused him to be flooded with feelings of loss. This accounted for the depth of his depression. It also did not help that he had been drinking heavily every day for the past 6 months to "keep him from thinking about it and help him blot out the pain."

Old wounds, current life stressors, and chemical dependence. A very familiar pattern. Roger admitted that he was too traumatized at the time to grieve the loss of his parents. He lived with his aunt and uncle until he went to college. No one ever said anything to him. He went through it alone and did what he knew how to do. He coped by shutting down his feelings, and going about his business. Then, 30 years later the wound is opened by a parallel experience.

Roger has several simultaneous issues, as is usually the case. He has his old wounds, current life stressors, and his alcohol dependence. He also has his wife's grief to deal with and the way it is stressing their relationship. He also has impending financial chaos if he does not get back to work.

The first thing that needs to be done in a crisis is to develop a strategy. The first rule is that you don't work on old wounds when you are trying to survive. Crisis management dictates just that. We focused on specific goals of coping daily with his feeling too overwhelmed to work. He established daily schedules and tasks which made him feel more in control. He stopped drinking which was a major task in itself because it was a significant crutch. I had him focus more on self-caring strategies such as getting his support from friends and outside sources rather than depending on his wife who was totally involved in a hospice program with her mother.

Finally, I had him discuss with his wife the problems he was having in order to reestablish communication. Crises of this magnitude often result in couples withdrawing from each other and getting self-preoccupied. They also withdraw and harbor resentment toward their partner for "not taking care of them".

Roger has a lot of healing to do in a lot of different areas. It is difficult to know where to start. I find it interesting how similar the grieving and recovery process are. In his case, he began with his shattered denial. Then he became very depressed, and he also struggled with acceptance and anger. He did a lot of bargaining and tried to find a way around the problem by avoidance and deadening the pain. He is in the stage of actively processing everything which will eventually lead to acceptance. This last stage will not come until his mother-in-law dies then he can continue his grieving of other old wounds. I keep trying to get him focused on the journey by staying in the moment. One step at a time in this case literally means taking one thing at a time on a daily basis. His journey of inner healing has begun with the shattering of his carefully constructed defenses. It has forced him to confront the inauthentic way he had been living his life. Now in this crisis he has an opportunity to heal and live more authentically. The wound is the messenger, how we respond will determine whether we begin the hero's journey of healing or continue the path to self-destruction. They are both a journey.

**NOTES**

# Meditation 3

The road to recovery always goes through the wasteland. In every great hero story we also observe the same phenomenon. Why is this? I think it is because the struggle increases our awareness, causes us to tap and develop inner resources and to search for new ways of doing and being. Let's look at some of the processes which are involved in our wasteland experiences.

In the first place, when we are in the wasteland, very often it is because we are wasted, or have wasted our resources. This word "waste" has so many connotations: it can mean, "excrement", "wilderness", "garbage", "consume", or "squander". I do not think it is any accident that this term is often used in connection with the experience of addiction or being high, or the consequences of addiction. It is a waste of potential and of life. A person is wasted when they use. It does turn a person's life into a wilderness when they are addicted. You do feel like excrement when you are used up.

This was the predicament I found myself in after my divorce. I was depressed, my financial affairs were in chaos, and my internal life was without any purpose, meaning or significance. I felt nothing, cared about nothing, and believed in nothing. I was a dead man walking. I was going through the motions. This was the consequence of my previous wounds and my failure to find authentic solutions.

Let me share with you some of the lessons I learned in my time in the wilderness. The first thing I discovered was my emotional deadness. And how empty and meaningless my life had become. This is an important point as I have stated many times before. In the classic hero stories this is the beginning of wisdom. In the biblical story of the prodigal son there is a phrase which I find highly illuminating. After the prodigal has wasted all of his resources, "in riotous living", he is working on a pig farm. For a wealthy jewish boy, this is a symbol of ultimate degradation. He looks about at his condition. The narrative reports, "he came to himself" and looked about as if to say, "what have I done to myself". This is the first lesson, **Recognition.** We must see fully what we have done. This leads to ownership and responsibility. Nothing can happen until this first step occurs. "We recognize that we are powerless".

The second lesson learned was that in order to heal my wounds I must **Reconnect.** Since I was a dead man, felt nothing and cared about nothing, it was imperative that I regain contact with me. This is probably the most difficult part of healing. We must feel the feelings, process them and work them through. Part of this struggle is also with remembering things which were blocked and disconnected. This means that the wound or wounds have to be addressed. This is where the inner struggle takes place in all hero journeys: it is always with ourselves. The struggle is to feel and heal or to avoid and run and continue being wasted.

This struggle leads naturally to the next lesson learned. Healing involves **Reconciliation.** Reconciliation must occur at many levels. We must first reconcile our inner conflicts, splits and fragmented memories. This restores our relationship with ourselves. Next comes reconciling our relationships with others.

And finally we must reconcile ourselves to life. This again is no easy task and involves the considerable work of inner healing. Coming to grips with our personal histories, who we are, our life situation, our ideas about life, our expectations and shattered illusions (faith system) leads to the next phase of our journey.

*Rebuilding* also has many levels and ramifications. In fact, we may look at the entire process of recovery as rebuilding. However, I want to emphasize the reconstructive aspects of this domain. Typically the consequences of being wasted is to have our lives in disarray, or chaos. I believe the familiar term for this is "wreckage of the past". Taking responsibility, taking control, and bringing order out of chaos is also a protracted process. As I did this I began to feel less overwhelmed. A simple example: I had let unopened mail pile up in the living room for several months. I began to open it piece by piece and make tough decisions. I confronted rather than avoided the problems. As I did this I began to feel better about myself. That is the net effect of inner healing and going through the wasteland. We are restored to ourselves, we regain our lives and self-esteem and reap the benefit of feeling more alive, competent and whole. This is the recovery process as I discovered it in my life: **the four r's of recovery. Recognize, reconnect, reconcile and rebuild.** All of this is the direct result of thrashing about in the wasteland.

# Meditation
# 4

    The gloom was so thick it felt like a huge, wet, black wool blanket. Mike just sat there, he looked pale and lifeless. His depression was shutting down all of his systems. He had just been to see his doctor and had been given the usual antibiotics for an infection. Mike's world had been collapsing for several months, he was at that point where everything had come together at one time. His court appearance for settlement of the divorce, IRS was pressuring him for back taxes, and his bankruptcy hearing had all occurred in a one week period. His body was reflecting the level of stress as it always does. Mike was reaping the whirlwind. The wreckage of his past was catching up with him all at once. Cocaine, sexual addiction, spending addiction, lack of management of his income all had created an abyss into which he had fallen.

    He asked me in a moment of self-pity, why is life so hard? There is a residual of protest even when we are trying to accept responsibility for our lives. A part of us wants to play the victim, and feel like life has been mean to us. This feeling comes from our wounded narcissism which believes that the world ought to bow down before us and pave our paths with riches and adulation. It is very painful and overwhelming when the consequences of our choices hit us all at once. For Mike, rebuilding does not seem like an option. His suicidal thinking and despair reflect a hopelessness and helplessness that he feels when he contemplates his situation at the moment. Yet, this is precisely the moment he has needed to get to. This is the moment where the Phoenix can rise from the ashes.

Mike and I have been working together long enough for me to be able to say things to him and for him to trust me enough to hear me. The only message I have for him is one that has come from my own experience. In my darkest hour I reached out and began to work. That was the moment in which my rebuilding began. For me the analogy which seems to fit the best is that of remodeling a house. It is very difficult to live in one which is completely torn up. In order for us to restore a house we first need a plan. Secondly we need competent help, and thirdly we need to do the work.

Restoration must take into account the structural integrity of the original structure. Unfortunately as humans we can't scrap this model and move to a palace in the suburbs. This is a given. We always start from where we are with what we have. There is so much work to do that many people don't know where to start so they feel like giving up. The only place you can start is by understanding the process which got you where you are. The rest comes after the inventory. Self-esteem, fractured relationships, finances, our bodies, emotional scars, old wounds, legal difficulties become a part of the restoration. Obviously, we can't solve all of the problems all at once. This is the part that is not glamorous and doesn't appeal to our infantile egos. I want all of this to go away: right now! I don't want to pay the price of my bad judgment, impulsivity, and irresponsibility. I want to be forgiven and have the bad stuff go away. It takes years to straighten out the consequences of living badly. The good news in this is that as we pay off one creditor after another our self-esteem and sense of integrity grow. As we restore old relationships and build new ones we build ourselves a new room in the house. We must have some place of sanctuary when the task becomes too difficult. We need support and encouragement to help us through the dark nights when we see no end and have no faith for the journey.

This is perhaps the greatest lesson, build first a context of hope and faith which will sustain you in the rebuilding project. The rest is just hard work that needs to be guided by an intelligent plan. Take pleasure from the gains and focus on the process. Let the negative history go. Self-respect comes when you earn it inch by inch. If you focus on the process of recovery you will be more likely to keep focused on what you are trying to do with your life. This involves creating an entirely new measure of self-esteem. What will it take for you to be able to live with you? What will it take for you to be able to affirm and love you? Rebuilding finally comes down to rebuilding the fractured relationship with ourselves. This takes the rest of our lives, but what else is there to do? If we rebuild the internal structures of our lives with care and compassion the rest will take care of itself.

# 2

# SELF-ESTEEM

In this section we will explore the relationship between self-esteem and addiction. We will see that self-esteem is a crucial part of identity which comes from within and reflects deeply held feelings and attitudes. In other words, self-esteem is the kind of relationship one has with oneself. Its relationship to addiction stems from the fact that low self-esteem comes from deficiency, a feeling of emptiness that leads to a compulsive need to latch onto something external which will provide, often temporarily, a sense of competence and fulfillment. The quest to fill the inner emptiness may become tinged with anxiety and lead to desperate, repetitive, habitual behaviors which are the leading factors in addiction.

In this sense, the psychological basis of addiction is an attachment to something or someone outside yourself that you have developed to fill the void. Frequently, people substitute a preoccupation with things, substances, food, work, or sexual activity for healthy human relationships. These activities are substitutes for that which leads to feelings of power, control, significance and meaning. And as such, they give only temporary satisfaction; they don't lead to an inner feeling of self-esteem. I once had a client who said to me, "have you ever been hungry for something and you didn't know what it was? I've tried drugs, alcohol, sex and food and I still have this hunger!" This is an example of what I am writing about, the hunger for self-esteem which often leads to addiction when it is not authentically fulfilled.

If low self-esteem leads to addiction, then it stands to reason that working on the real problem is a necessary and healthy antidote. Building healthy self-esteem means developing confidence and strength from within, in essence, of learning to have control over things which directly affect self-esteem. By gaining a feeling of being O.K. within yourself, the basis of self-esteem is no longer external. As such, it is more stable and enduring over time. Finally, it means cultivating a respectful, compassionate, accepting and intimate friendship with yourself. Often, it is difficult to know which comes first, addiction and then low self-esteem or vice versa. Not everyone with low self-esteem becomes an addict. Let us say, then, that low self-esteem, along with several other factors we have already discussed, play a significant role in creating a vulnerability to addiction. And we may say, with a high degree of certainty, that an eventual casualty of addiction is loss of self-esteem.

In this section your only task is to read the essays, meditate on them and pay attention to any memories, images, feelings or thoughts which arise from your conversation with me. Then write them down and anything else which comes to mind. This process I call journaling. It is a technique that all spiritual travelers have used throughout the ages. Think of it as a trip log. The writing will not only preserve the record of your journey but it will also help you to perhaps reconnect with feelings which have been repressed or disconnected. The result will be that you will feel more connected and grounded in your own experience and subsequently more alive and whole. This is the essence of regaining self-esteem. Finally, I should note that this process of self-discovery is also a very effective antidote for dealing with any form of compulsive behavior because it disrupts the process. Unconscious drives are replaced with conscious awareness. Disconnected needs and feelings are reconnected and felt in a way which can lead to more authentic behavior. Blind repetitive behavior is now guided by awareness and choice. Fear, guilt, shame. and anger which often fuel a compulsion are replaced by tolerance, compassion, and acceptance. With the intensity and conflict reduced, the compulsion loses its power. Thus behavior can be more consciously and freely directed into channels which build self-esteem.

**NOTES**

# Meditation

# 1

Self-esteem has joined a host of pop psychology terms to become a 90's buzzword. Talk shows, books and self-help guru's have saturated our consciousness to the point that our conversations seem to revolve around whether someone does or does not feel good about themselves. This level of familiarity causes us to take self-esteem for granted: we assume that we all mean the same thing when we use the term. In this series of meditations I will be writing about the relationship between self-esteem, addiction, and recovery. My intention is to discuss them in ways that will generate awareness and self-understanding which I hope will become translated into transformation and healing. I have found guided meditation to be a very meaningful experience that is foundational to the recovery journey.

What is self-esteem? It is not something we are born with. Nor is it some fixed commodity that we either have or don't have. In the psychological sense, self-esteem refers to many complex attitudes, thoughts, feelings and behaviors which all refer to the Self. In my view, self-esteem is the defining relationship we have with ourselves, with others and with the world. In essence, self-esteem is our sense of identity: it is who we are. It is out of his sense of self that we live. Understood in this manner, self-esteem functions as a self-fulfilling prophecy.

In essence, If I value myself, am realistic in my self-appraisal, accept myself, feel that my life has meaning, significance and purpose, feel competent in my dealings with the world and relate in a compassionate way with others, then my self-esteem is probably pretty good. The hallmark of self-esteem is that it does not permit abuse, victimization or engage in self-destructive behavior.

Conversely, one who is low in self-esteem, generally is self-critical, feels inferior and incompetent, is self-rejecting and usually has difficulty in loving and being loved. Victimization and self-destructive behavior are indicative of low self-esteem.

Clearly, people with high self-esteem think, feel and behave very differently from those with self-esteem problems. In my 20 years as a therapist, I have come to believe that restoring self-esteem is critical to recovery. In order to recover, we need to know where the damage is, how it is affecting current behavior and what needs to change. In essence, we need to do an accurate appraisal of the problem.

The origins of self-esteem are found in our earliest encounters with parents, teachers, peers and family: all play powerful roles. In fact, it is safe to say that self-esteem is the byproduct of all of our experiences.

The early years are crucial to the development of self-esteem because we are the most vulnerable and dependent at that time. It is the foremost task of parents to nurture the emerging self of the child. As children we internalize parental attitudes toward us. Through imitation and reward we learn about the world and our place in it. We come to treat ourselves the way others have treated us. In these years of rapid development, the issues of self-esteem revolve around **attachment, autonomy, competence, meaning, significance and a sense of worth.** The entire thrust of development is to acquire a sense of mastery in our interactions with the world. Furthermore, all of our interactions are based on the development of a cohesive, consistent and meaningful world view. We must learn the rules of the game as we play. Finally, through our relationships with others, we learn our significance to them. *Our basic sense of worth is tied up in these three things: competence, meaning and significance.*

Self-esteem is the consequence of all these early encounters. Once it is formed, it tends to remain stable and predictable over time unless affected by trauma or crisis.

Self-esteem, since it is a product of our continual interaction with the world, is always at risk. There are a number of factors which may create a crisis of self-esteem. Trauma, loss of a significant person, illness, failure, inability to accomplish goals or to establish nurturant life circumstances over a long period of time, abusive relationships and failed dreams may all negatively impact self-esteem. Certainly, addiction meets the conditions for impacting self-esteem in a disastrous way.

In short, anything that threatens self-esteem may cause anxiety. Anything which is lost that was important to our sense of worth creates loss and depression. Prolonged conditions which result in being demeaned may cause us to suffer permanent damage in the area of our self-esteem. Abusive relationships and self-destructive behavior lead to conditions of victimization. These are toxic to positive self-esteem. It is under these conditions that a person may be ripe for addiction.

In my experience, people are addiction-prone because of three risk factors: Genetic predisposition (biological traits), psychological vulnerability (trauma, stress, family history), and current stressors. None of us have perfect histories. We are all walking wounded with self-esteem vulnerabilities. The key issue here is that when we feel empty, have difficulty feeling good about ourselves and experience significant levels of loneliness, anxiety, depression, guilt or boredom, we may discover that something, someone or some activity may help us feel better. If we connect with these outside factors, we are ripe for addiction.

Anything which reduces anxiety, depression or emptiness while at the same time helps us feel more confident, more in control and more attractive (even for a moment) has the potential to be addictive. The key to transformation lies in finding things which solve these problems authentically. In short, solutions which work!

**NOTES**

# Meditation
# 2

Hitting bottom is like finding oneself in a wasteland without a compass. Though a natural consequence of addiction it is often thought of as the worst possible moment in a person's life. It is, but it may also be the best, providing it leads to transformation. Like all moments of crisis, it depends on what our response is that determines the rest of the journey. Hitting bottom is definitely a crossroads, a gateway experience.

Self-esteem is one of the first casualties of addiction. Restoring self-esteem, therefore must be the foundation for any recovery program. In this essay I will look at the problem of self-hatred and suggest how to go about living with ourselves in a way that leads to healthy self-esteem.

For many, guilt and remorse are appropriate emotions. It is normal to look at the wreckage of our lives and feel badly. We ought to feel that way about the shattered relationships, the financial chaos, the broken trust, the career that is destroyed, the way we have wasted our talents, abilities, bodies and minds because these are all the very real consequences of addiction.

This week I had another reminder of this very problem. I had to deal with a legal suit brought against me because of a decision, a bad one, I made ten years ago. This encounter triggered all kinds of feelings; anger, incompetence, stupidity, self-hatred, helplessness, and hopelessness. I spent a whole week revisiting my past and recounting a whole litany of mistakes. I have spent the last ten years trying to rebuild my life, and just when I thought I was beginning to get on top of things and get the wreckage cleared away, I was confronted once more by my past. After a week of self-reproach I decided to take the advise I have been handing out to my clients and forgive myself. How do we go about this?

The first step is *awareness*. This is the antidote to denial. The function of hitting bottom is to penetrate our denial. In order to accomplish any kind of meaningful change we must admit that there is a problem. The second step is *ownership*. We must take responsibility for creating the problem. I did it! One of the primary reasons for denial is that we don't like to face our pain and our problems. We are escape artists of the first magnitude. Houdinis! Living with awareness is painful. It can be really depressing looking at our lives and the mistakes we have made. It is very natural to not want to look at it. The fact is, however is that nothing can happen until we accept that there is a problem and that it originated with us. Recovery will never happen as long as we blame everyone else for the condition of our lives. Victims seldom change if they continue to blame. The good news about awareness is that eventually we feel more alive and are better able to live with greater intelligence. If we give ourselves permission to feel and to see then we are ready to take the next step: *Assessment*.

This is a very important step because it leads to self-understanding and eventually forgiveness. I am talking about a special kind of assessment. In this kind it is important to suspend judgment. By assessment I mean looking at our lives in a way that is directed towards understanding the process by which we arrived at our predicament. By looking at our lives through the lens of self-hatred and self-condemnation we do not allow ourselves to ask the important question. How did this happen to me? When we focus on looking realistically at the evolution of the problem then we will be on the way to understanding ourselves. Meaningful change cannot come about until we really understand the problem.

Understanding is the first stage of empowered recovery. In looking at ourselves with suspended judgment we need to cultivate an attitude, a perspective, a way of looking at ourselves which will lead to acceptance. This attitude I call **compassion.** It does no good to go around daily and beat ourselves over the head for all of our mistakes. This leads to depression, lowered self-esteem and usually relapse. The key here is to develop more realistic expectations for ourselves. And a more compassionate attitiude when we do find ourselves failing to live up to our expectatins.

Once you have acquired some awareness and have begun the journey towards self-understanding you are ready to take the next step: *targeting.* What do I mean? It is very hard to change if we do not have an idea about what it is we want to change. It is like wanting to go on a trip and not having a destination. As we have been acquiring an understanding of the problem and finding out what gets us into trouble we should be seeing what we need to do about it. Targeting merely means to focus on small, achievable goals for change. This is what I believe is meant by one step at a time. Pick a problem, develop a strategy for change, a meaningful goal, and then work the program.

The next step follows naturally, in order to improve self-esteem and feel better about ourselves we need to have an image of how we want to be. I encourage my clients to engage in a process called *visualization*. Spend a few moments each day visualizing yourself living the kind of life you could feel good about. It can't happen if we can' imagine it.

The next step is to put our action plan into motion. I call this *enactment*. This will lead to empowered recovery. We are acting in a way that will lead to more intelligent, aware, considered, chosen, self-conscious living. This is the very essence of self-esteem. Feeling that I matter and that what I do matters builds self-esteem. Feeling that I have the power to live my life in a way that leads to self-respect builds self-esteem.

The journey to self-esteem begins with the wound and requires going through the wasteland of self-hatred and self-doubt. It means that we will feel the full weight of our self-destructiveness, the guilt of wrongdoing, the regret of wasted life, the despair of failure, wrong choices, disillusionment and the emptiness of it all. We will feel the regret of lost love and shattered relationships and the loneliness of having alienated our friends and loved ones. This is the meaning of the wasteland. This journey is always an inward one. No one can do it but us. But it does not have to be alone. There is a whole host of fellow travelers: a community of people who have been there and are searching for common answers to common questions and sharing their wisdom, strength and hope. The heroes journey requires courage: heroics. But the redemption and healing which comes from our effort will lead to greater self-esteem. Keep the faith!

# Meditation

## 3

I am often curious when people use a word or a phrase to describe what is happening with them. Often it is the current pop psycho-babble which sounds good when it is rolling off the tongue but does not really convey much information. I was amused the other day when I was caught in full flight with a big time cliche which I used with a client. He was comfortable enough to ask me what I meant by that. In this case the cliche was "You gotta be true to yourself." I threw out a few more well chosen phrases, all equally as meaningless and then caught myself. I told him I would talk to him about it next week. Just what, exactly are we trying to say when we tell someone to be true to themselves?

The first thing which comes to my mind is that we are indicating a kind of relationship we want the other person to have with him/herself. But what kind of relationship? What I realized with my client's question was that he genuinely did not have a clue about what I meant because it was foreign to his experience. He had grown up in a family where people were not true to themselves or to each other. The quality most missing was respect for each member of the family. No one had taught him to respect himself by doing it. Respect means to have high regard for your own existence. And when you do this you also act respectfully toward the other person's experience. When we act respectfully we are trying to affirm and preserve the other's self-esteem. I say this over and over: it is the sacred duty of every parent to safeguard their child's sense of self-esteem.

We must also convey to our children that we trust them. In doing this we are teaching them to value themselves. Trust is the cornerstone of self-esteem as well as all relationships. We build trust by encouraging them to try new experiences and by exploring and developing their talents. Finally, we teach them trust by holding them responsible for themselves, their decisions and their actions. There are a whole host of studies that support this idea that democratic parents, those who teach their children how to make decisions and share decision making with them, raise children with much higher self-esteem than parents who tell their children to "do it because I said so."

I did not start this with the intent of this "being a how to create self-esteem in children" but it seems to be ending up this way. Perhaps it is because we are trying to find out what it means to be true to yourself. And in fact restoring our own self-esteem is much like the process of reparenting children.

Another quality which is important for being true to oneself is caring. Again, this is something we that develops in our formative years. If we felt loved, respected, trusted, and valued as children we probably are not going to have problems with self-esteem. This seems to be the big stumbling block for people in recovery. Caring about ourselves gets blocked by **shame and guilt.** I had a young woman the other day sit in my office and engage in a tirade against herself because she had made a mistake at work. She chastised, belittled and demeaned herself: finally, I stopped her and inquired about what she was doing. She responded by saying that she needed to do that so she would not make that mistake again. It is evident that she didn't trust herself to behave correctly without continuously criticizing herself. The net effect of this sort of self-criticism is to create depression and lower self-esteem. I asked her how she would treat a young child who had made a mistake. She said she would try to explain to the child what was wrong and what the correct behavior ought to be. She said she would not treat the child the way she treats herself.

Being true to ourselves also means to have a sense of Identity. We need to have an idea of who it is we are being true to. In this way our behavior will be consistent with the Image of our self. Integrity comes from consistency with values. When we build a large structure we want all of the components to fit together in a way that they serve the whole. If they don't then the building will not have integrity and won't be very strong. So, being true to ourselves seems to involve making choices that will help us be the kind person we think we are trying to become. Certainly one of the more devastating consequences of addiction is damaged self-esteem for this very reason. We make choices which are against our best interest, violate all of the principles of healthy relationships and are not consistent with being true to ourselves.

Being true to ourselves comes down to loving ourselves. For it is in loving that we achieve the highest state of being human. And we do this by being faithful to our best sense of what that means at this very moment in life.

# Meditation

# 4

I attended a "Recovery Event" the other day; it was to promote drug and alcohol awareness in students. There were a number of celebrities present and several awards were given for being M.V.P.'s. As I heard the celebrities talk of their addiction and recovery, it got me to wondering about what it takes to be somebody. I found great irony in the celebrities who had become somebody and were utterly unhappy. Isn't this what most people want? Fame, celebrity, money, attention, success, power: aren't these our definitions of what we think it would take to make us somebody?

It is this very irony that is at the heart of addiction. The desperate desire to be somebody comes from a black hole in the personality where self-esteem should be. Unhappiness and feelings of being a nobody are the seeds of striving which lead to overdriven pursuit of attention and adulation. Feelings of inferiority drive some to crave power and fame, to have others tell them they really are somebody.

Again, we see the irony. When people with low self-esteem accomplish something they experience guilt. "I don't deserve this. If others tell me I am wonderful, I don't believe them because I know the real truth about me." So drugs and alcohol become props for emptiness and anxiety about being somebody who is nobody just like all the other nobodies fantasizing about being somebody. Probably, somebodies fantasizes about being nobody for a day. When expectations exceed the ability to perform there is usually disappointment. When low self-esteem is the problem one can never be rich enough, famous enough, or powerful enough. Is this all there is?, becomes the lament of the chronically empty.

What does it take to be somebody? Who decides when I am somebody? When I turned 40, I was deeply depressed. It hit me, I was a failure. I was miserable, I hadn't accomplished anything: I felt. In therapy I finally came to terms with my expectations and the dynamics of my failed attempts to be somebody. I was a failed 'wanna be.

Being somebody is a deeply felt need in all of us. It is the foundation of our self-esteem. In fact, self-esteem is just a shorthand way of talking about the need to feel significant, to feel a sense of competence, to feel a part of a community, to be self-reliant, to have others value and respect us and to have a caring relationship with ourselves. If, in our development, we have managed to accomplish these stages then we have a sense of worth or high self-esteem. The reason I was so unhappy at age 40 had more to do with an abusive, alcoholic father and a very needy mother than it did with what was going on in my life at the time. In fact, my unhappiness was symptomatic that I did not have a good relationship with myself. All that I had accomplished didn't mean anything to me.

I watched the film "Quiz Show" the other night. It was directed by Robert Redford. It helped me look at how we get seduced by society. Charles Van Doren came from a famous family, he had everything, his father was successful, his mother was successful; he seemingly had it all.

In a climatic, wonderfully powerful speech, he recounted his fall. He was seduced because he was a 'wanna be. "I stood on other people's shoulders and I flew too high on borrowed wings". What did he mean? To me, it seemed he was talking about never having learned to feel good about himself. He was somebody's son, he lived up to the aspirations of others and hadn't done anything he felt really good about. He was seduced by money, having his picture on Time Magazine and hanging out with famous people. He asks us, "What would you do?"

Well, certainly the promise of all these instant solutions to our problem of being in the world is seductive isn't it? This is the core of addiction: instant gratification, instant escape from the problems of living, and easy access to power, fame, money and acclaim. All this and we don't even have to do anything, we can have it all; we can fly as high as we want on borrowed wings. There is one small clause in the fine print of the contract, however. But who reads contracts anyway, let alone the fine print, right?

The fine print says all we have to do is make a small down payment with our integrity and make regular payments with our self-esteem. And, oh yes, there's a large balloon payment at the end of the contract which doesn't have a specified number of payments. The balloon payment? Self-esteem, health, relationships, friends, family and career will be forfeited on demand.

The road to self-esteem is not necessarily the same as the road to being somebody. It may in fact go in an entirely different direction. The choice seems simple enough, but obviously, if it were that simple everyone would love themselves and it would be a great world. Flying on our own wings is the antidote to the problem posed by "Quiz Show." What does this mean? First, we start with what is. We are, who we have become. What's the matter with being you? Does this sound familiar? We start with an inventory. We get honest about who we are. This inventory must also include assets, resources and strengths as well as the litany of failure.

Once you have assessed honestly and clearly where you are, the next step is to determine whether you like where you are and who you are: If not, why not? Self-esteem is a matter of valuations. What do you value most in life? What is your ultimate concern?

The reason I believe self-esteem is about values is because we seem to become what we value. What we become is a function of choices and commitments. These are a function of what we care about.

If you decide you don't like you and where you are in your life, then you may want to make changes. What kind of changes? That depends on the kind of person you want to be. What kind of person do you need to be in order to love and respect yourself?

The next step is learning to fly. In order to learn to fly, you need to learn as much as you can about yourself and the art of living. The other component is learning to trust your own wings and skills that you are developing as a novice pilot. Flying solo on your own wings is, finally, a greater rush than trying to be somebody. Discovering this is probably the most difficult thing I have ever learned. Somehow flying looks so easy. And maybe, if I could get on the cover of "People" magazine or win a Pulitzer, or. . . . .

# 3

# ADDICTION

Psychological dependence occurs when a person uses chemicals which are psycho-active. That is to say, they change consciousness and alter mood in one way or another. Over time, the chemically dependent person relies increasingly on a change in feeling or consciousness to cope more effectively with self, reality, or others. Most people gain some pleasure or immediate benefit from consuming chemicals. This is the reason for using them. I believe addicts have learned to self-medicate. If the results were immediately painful or did nothing, there would be no reason for their use. Chemicals are powerfully reinforcing because they have an immediate effect that may be both physically and psychologically pleasurable, as well as socially encouraged and supported.

Becoming chemically dependent is a seductive, tricky business and it affects everyone differently. Each person is at risk in seemingly hundreds of various ways. I want to help you understand the process of becoming chemically dependent.

Physiological addiction is acquired through different channels than psychological dependence. The mechanism is very complex and we do not need to go into all of the technical reasons now. In simple terms, the body, because it is wonderfully adept at meeting the demands of adaptation, begins to set in motion the necessary chemical changes to handle your chemical intake. As you put in more chemicals, your body works harder to adapt to the new level of intake. Gradually, over time, it requires more chemicals to get the original benefit of whatever is used. When this is coupled with the increased psychological dependence, a very powerful compulsion to use is set in motion.

Addicts come from all levels of education, socioeconomic classes, and ethnic groups, but, have the common bond of their problem. This commonality of problems is the reason for the approach I have adopted in my treatment programs. I believe that addiction is a problem with multiple causes (biological, psychological, and social). This multiple causality is perhaps made worse or triggered by life stress. When the addiction prone person becomes physically addicted and psychologically dependent, there are powerful social learning factors that sustain the problem. Addiction is a high cost behavior. That is, the consequences lead to damage in many different areas. The most obvious ones are health and loss of job. The higher costs, though, are to self-esteem and damage to those we love.

Addiction eventually leads to the natural consequence of shame and self-contempt. Not only does the addict come to feel that way about himself, but of course, others feel the same way as well. Besides the problems of self-esteem, there is a whole constellation of related problems: poor communication, difficulty in interpersonal relationships, difficulty in dealing with feelings and poor coping skills under stress. Because addicts have similarities in problems, I believe that the most effective recovery program is one that teaches skills for living.

My fundamental conviction is that by increasing feelings of competency and interpersonal effectiveness this will lead to gains in self-esteem and more successful relationships. If we feel better about ourselves, and others, then the need to use mind altering chemicals will decrease correspondingly. The goal is to build a practical skill base through learning and practice.

In sum, addiction is a complex problem requiring changes at many levels. Addicts have been found to have a shared cluster of problems. These problems include poor coping skills, low self-esteem, difficulties in interpersonal relationships, difficulty in communication, problems in recognizing, experiencing and expressing feelings, inability to experience intimacy in love relationships, and dysfunctional family lives.

The life of an addict who, by definition, is chemically dependent on a mind altering substance, is characterized by two things: disintegration and bondage. Psychological, physical, economic, social, career, and family problems abound: this is the downward cycle of disintegration. Secondly, the life of addiction is one of bondage because the addict has formed a coercive bond with a substance. The addict comes to experience life as slavery, typified by torturous periods of lack of control. Like Humpty Dumpty, all the King's horses and all the King's men cannot put him back together again. Unlike Humpty Dumpty, however, the addict need not be a passive victim who is destined to being perpetually shattered. The key in the equation is the addict. If you are motivated, willing to participate in your own recovery, given adequate resources and a caring and supportive recovery environment, you can recover. You can regain your lost power. The strategy for recovery in this program is based on the belief that addiction is a complex disorder that has its roots in the physical, emotional, psychological, social, and family history of each unique individual.  Although addicts share a common affliction, each is unique in response to the problem.

The problem must be confronted now!  Denial, that deadly defense, must be penetrated and discarded.  Honesty with yourself and others will restore the lost respect and self-esteem that are the first casualties of addiction.

**NOTES**

# Meditation

# 1

Self-esteem and substance abuse are so intertwined it is difficult to know which comes first. Does someone with low self-esteem use drugs and alcohol to feel better about themselves? Probably. Does someone who abuses chemicals experience a certain loss of self-esteem? Most definitely!

I have a client, a young woman in her mid-twenties who just celebrated her 1st birthday. She was addicted to crank for 5 years. As she so often told me, "at first I was using it, it was not using me." After losing her job, ending an abusive relationship, and experiencing all kinds of financial havoc, she decided she might have a problem. "It was me, I had lost control of my life. I was sexually promiscuous, harassed by creditors and had to avoid my family, I hated my life." All of this she divulged one day in a session.

This certainly illustrates that substance abuse can and usually does have a devastating effect on a person's self-esteem. The loss of control, ruined relationships, lost jobs, deteriorating health, and financial chaos are all so familiar to those who have been down that road. The phrase "wreckage of the past" so aptly describes this condition. And that is exactly what it is. Those who have lived to tell their stories know the all to familiar feeling that goes with taking responsibility for the damage. Remorse and self-hatred.

I did this. Such a simple phrase with so much riding on it. When we admit it we feel the full weight of our own self-destructiveness. Why would someone do this? It is such a high cost adventure!

In Beth's case, the seeds of her own self-destruction are pretty clear. She was the second child in a family and was adopted. She was sexually molested by her older brother. She kept it a secret. She started experimenting with drugs in high school. When she left home for college she felt lost, confused and alienated. She dropped out of college and discovered the party scene. Sexuality, having a good time, and methamphetamines all came together for her at the same time. This powerful combination coupled with her vulnerability set the stage for her addiction.

This in my view, is the key. It is our vulnerability in the area of self-esteem. It is my conviction that anything which fosters an enhanced sense of self, i.e., makes us feel powerful, significant, important, sexual or loved has the potential for addiction. And the converse is also true. Anything which helps us to escape feeling inadequate, inferior, incompetent, insignificant, unwanted, depressed, anxious, isolated, or unloved also has the power to become addictive.

My client said to me the other day after a year and a half of therapy, "I am building the kind of life I can respect." We both sat there in utter silence, the kind of silence in which both people know something very significant has just happened. We let it hang there for a few moments, this very tangible feeling she and I both had. It was a sense that she had just recognized how far she had come in putting her life back together. We both smiled. We knew!

There is a very real consequence to self-esteem that comes from taking that first step. A step which began six months after beginning to see me. Her original-presenting problem was depression and the issue of incest. It took her six months to admit to me she had a drug problem. Since she made that admission it has been easier for her to face a number of other problems squarely. She has had to deal with tremendous anger at her brother, anger at her original mother for abandoning her, and anger at her adoptive mother for being critical and non-supportive, anger at her boyfriend's abuse and finally, anger at herself for the mess she had made of things. The irony in all of this, of course, is that her anger at others got translated into self-destructive behavior. Another seeming paradox, we are angry at others so we take it out on ourselves..

Beth's recovery has been underscored by her struggle to respect herself on her terms. We have continually focused every decision within the framework of whether or not this decision would help her achieve her goal of being able to respect herself. From this goal of self-respect has evolved a life strategy. It has changed the arena of her struggle from trying to live on mom and dad's terms and pleasing them to her own arena in which she is defining herself.

This has resulted in a new job that she enjoys. She enjoys it because she is showing up, doing the work and getting appropriate recognition for work well done. She has returned to college because she wants to. She is in a monogamous relationship because she wants to be. She is deeply struggling with the aftermath of incest. The fear of intimacy, ambivalence, guilt for wanting her own needs met, suffocating dependency, and lack of trust all surface because she is not using crank.

In short, she has become a woman of substance in her own eyes.

She is substantial and therefore is no longer reliant on substances. Self-esteem, for her, is the natural outcome of living a life she is becoming proud of. Is her struggle over? Is her recovery complete? In actuality it has just begun. It is just that she now understands what the issues are and what she needs to do to keep her recovery going in the right direction.

The journey is and always has been about self-esteem. Whether we face ourselves, find the authentic voice within, listen to our deepest needs, live with courage and make the commitment to create a quality life is the most important issue we will ever face. It is in fact our prsonal heroics. To be the person I respect most can only come from me, not you. Sobering isn't it?

**NOTES**

# Meditation

# 2

They came to me in utter crisis. He was having several affairs, spending money like a drunken sailor and flying around the country. She was furious, depressed, frightened, and feeling devastated in her self-esteem. Yet, they called me and made an appointment; they wanted to work it out.

On the surface, this appeared to be the usual marital crisis of someone who had been married 12 years. They were bored, frustrated, unhappy, restless, and fed up. The usual maxim in therapy is that nothing is as it appears. In this case it was more than true. There were several layers of problems: his, hers, and theirs. These problems were surfacing all at the same time. That's the usual cause of a crisis: too many problems, all at once.

One of the primary issues for this couple was their dependency on each other for feelings of worth. Each had grown up under extensive conditions of abuse. She was sexually molested by a grandfather and abandoned by her mother. He had an abusive father and a mother who was a chronic invalid. He had to care for her and received little nurturance in return.

This is the legacy of abuse, low self-esteem, feelings of helplessness, and dependency on others for feelings of significance and worth. This often leads to having the self-image of a victim. It is also typical that out of all the people in the world these two people found each other: mirror images of their problems. Naturally, they fell in love and expected that they would live happily after; each filling the other's needs for self-esteem. It is true that self-esteem prospers when we are loved. The problem with low self-esteem from abuse is that we can never feel loved enough. When this happens the other becomes the persecutor.

This recurring drama of victim-persecutor had been going on for their whole marriage. The cycle of abusive relationships begins with a **"honeymoon" phase** and then progresses through a buildup of disappointment and resentment to an outburst of **anger** and perhaps violence. Then **remorse and penitence** occurs which then leads to another honeymoon phase. Some people play this game forever and we call it a stable abusive relationship. In some cases it may end in tragedy and death. In this particular case they found ways to smooth out the cycle. They found a marital aid. She discovered heroin and he cocaine. This was a wonderful discovery. For her it made the pain of her childhood disappear in a haze of euphoria. Her depression is only a dim memory when she uses. And most significantly, her sexual dysfunction because of early abuse magically goes away.

They are able to have terrific sexual encounters when she is high. In fact, he praises her for being the partner he has always wanted. She turns him on and he really loves it. When she is not so responsive he goes and finds someone else. She feels wonderful, loved, and taken away from all her cares; what more could she ask for? Better living through chemistry.

In his case, cocaine makes him feel omnipotent. He is an artist and feels creative when he uses. All of his friends do it and he feels supported and validated by this very hip crowd. The emptiness and loneliness of his childhood recede into the distant past in the rush of being high. And besides this, he and his wife have these magical sexual encounters when they get high together. What more could they ask for: young, hip, successful and turned on in a virtual reality world.

For some, this may seem like a familiar story. You may even know how it will end. But the couple in question doesn't know yet. Their marital aids-life aids still seem to be working. They help them function and experience life more intensely. The downside is still able to be managed by using again.

This is precisely the problem. Psycho-active chemicals do help us to have more energy. They do reduce pain and depression. They help us have more fun and reduce our inhibitions. They elevate our mood and make life seem wonderful. That's why they are called "psycho-active". They also, and here is the downside, create both physiological and psychological dependence. This dependence usually leads to tolerance and then addiction. In short, there is a cost to all the wonderful benefits. It is a predictable process, this road to addiction and abuse. As addiction increases the positive benefits are fewer and farther between. More is required to achieve the same old effect. It is the law of diminishing returns. As dependence increases, the negative consequences begin to pile up. Health, careers, friendships, relationships, family and self-esteem all seem to be chemically soluble. As dependence increases, self control and voluntary behavior decrease. The good news is that cocaine and heroin for this couple are the gateway to paradise. The bad news is that paradise ends up being hell.

In being seduced by the short term benefits of chemicals they are cheating themselves out of the joy of true intimacy that comes with effort, commitment, caring, trust and vulnerability. They won't discover the contentment of self-reliance and the joy of a well lived life. Working through old pain, facing and feeling depression and fear without chemicals is difficult. But the hard won benefit is wholeness. It isn't hip or cool in some circles. It doesn't create ecstasy and doesn't have the pounding excitement of a cocaine rush, but it does leave you with your soul intact.

Being able to live with oneself and live authentically is a joy that makes life worth living. It also becomes the foundation for friendship and lasting, loving, relationships.

And so this couple is working on bridging their fears, trying to establish trust and communicate their fear, anger and needs. This is hard work, and the temptation is always there to trip out on each other with just a little boost when it gets rough. The motivation to use is very powerful. They must find the motivation to play it straight by reaching down within themselves to a spiritual core. It becomes a question of values. What do they want?

**NOTES**

# Meditation

# 3

Addiction has many casualties. Self-esteem is one of them. This elusive something is also one of the most difficult to restore. Perhaps the question most frequently asked of me as a therapist is, "How can I learn to love myself when I have done so many stupid things?" It seems to me that answering this question is pivotal to recovery.

The recovery journey is the most difficult undertaking anyone will ever attempt. It begins with conditions much like those of war: we stand amidst the bombed out ruins of our lives. The aftermath of addiction leaves our bodies, relationships, careers friendships, families and psyches in shreds.

The inescapable conclusion once denial is pierced? I am the author of my own destruction! How, in the face of this stark conclusion, can I even begin to feel good about me?

The journey begins with the first step. We acknowledge that we have a problem. I have always been amazed at how much healing comes from facing reality. There is something about admitting the problem that creates a new reality based on honesty rather than denial.

This radical step creates a new relationship with ourselves as well as with others. Healing cannot begin without this step. I have a problem. It is I who has created all of this havoc! Implicit in this admission are the seeds of recovery. By making this discovery and admission, something else besides honesty is happening. We have stopped blaming and have taken responsibility.

"I did it," therefore, "I can undo it." This takes us out of the helpless victim role and places us on the threshold of empowerment. When we make this radical admission, we are also laying the groundwork for future steps. By admitting that I have a problem, I am also taking the first stumbling step toward self-acceptance. I do not like me at this step; it is very difficult to accept who I am, but acceptance of my full potential for destruction is a part of self-acceptance. Just like the moon, we have a dark side as well as the side we show to the public. Healing begins, not by rejecting our self-destructive impulses, but rather, by bringing them into the full light of consciousness. It's much easier to keep an eye on them this way also.

The fellowship of the 12 step community illustrates very well the point I am making. It is a community based on the dark side. No one goes to a meeting to be with others who are there to brag about how wonderful they are. The healing comes from exposing our flaws. The miracle happens when we experience acceptance from others.

I believe that this remarkable experience is the next crucial step in the process of restoring self-esteem. Acceptance from others is fundamental to the embryonic self-esteem we are trying to nurture. At this juncture in our recovery we are very much like newborn babies: fragile and vulnerable. We need support, feedback, guidance and most of all, the loving acceptance of others who have been down the road and have lived to tell about it. They also provide survival models.

There is another factor in gaining self-esteem that is related to the first step. In recognizing that we have a problem, we begin our efforts to turn our lives around. In this step, we make a commitment to ourselves to stop doing what we were doing that led to our downfall.

Again, this is a radical departure from the lifestyle of addiction. By channeling my energies into saving my life, I am validating myself. I am saying by my behavior that I am worth saving. This a very critical point. It is the first of many necessary steps in the process of learning to care for ourselves.

By stopping our self-destructive behaviors we are also giving ourselves less ammunition--we have less reason to hate ourselves. To paraphrase Forrest Gump, "Self-hatred is as self-hatred does." Herein is the miracle of self-respect. I hate myself because I am an addict. Turn the formula around and it becomes, I respect myself because I am recovering. Respect from others will follow.

Restoring self-esteem is accomplished through a series of small steps. It takes on the quality of a journey when we set a destination that orders our steps and gives them purpose, direction and meaning. Recovery is a lifetime journey. In the course of this journey, we learn and come to care for and respect ourselves. These are the building blocks of self-esteem.

Self-esteem based on addiction results in a self-image of "I am an addict." When we begin the road to recovery, we change the formulation to "I am an addict who is in recovery." This becomes the new attitude toward ourselves. If we keep this as the overall big picture, it shifts our self-evaluation from all of our past failures to a focus on the here and now. This is all that matters. I believe this is at the heart of "One day at a time." This becomes the foundation for healing wounded self-esteem.

A final comment by way of summary. The recovery journey is never without effort. At every step of the way, we encounter resistance. Recovery resistance comes from our own ambivalence about ourselves: our guilt, shame, anger, depression, self-hatred and desire to take the easy way out. Self-esteem, like all growth and progress comes only by overcoming resistance.

**NOTES**

# Meditation

# 4

Love and addiction, are sometimes found together, sometimes found as substitutes. Let's look at this complex relationship as it also relates to self-esteem. Love seems to be the magic potion, the elixir of life that enlivens with its power and impoverishes by its absence. What will we give, what price will we pay for this essence of life? Can it also be addictive? Can we become addicted as a reaction to the lack of love?

This issue comes into focus for us all at certain times of life: a crisis, failure, a blow to our self-esteem or critical loss. These events make us all aware of our vulnerability or impoverishment. Facing our pain can lead to growth and enrichment of our lives. A case in point is a young woman I have been working with who has a number of complex issues: drug addiction, incest, adoption and not surprisingly, problems with self-esteem. She made a disconcerting discovery the other day. Out on a date she was touched in a very sexual way. She reacted very strongly and put a stop to the advance. She was surprised for two reasons. The first was that it upset her and secondly that she put a stop to it. This was new territory for her. In our discussion it became evident that she was experiencing things differently. Previously, she had been quite promiscuous and used sex as a way of bartering for relationships. By putting a stop to unwanted sex she was listening to her feelings, validating her worth and asking him to respect her. This was an important marker of her growth.

Now, she no longer feels the compulsion to barter sex for love or undermine her self-esteem by violating her boundaries. This need to be loved is a universal and powerful need. We all want to be loved and desired by others. We have also felt that excruciating emptiness and desolation when we lose love. We have also probably found ourselves making bad decisions and doing things we didn't want to because we thought it would get the love we wanted. Love comes in many forms and has many price tags. How we meet our love needs is an important marker of our self-esteem.

Another client, a very successful young man who has done well in business triggered a relapse when his daughter went back to live with her mother. "She left and I walked right into the first bar, I felt lonely, needy and lost, like an abandoned child." These feelings are difficult to tolerate. Vulnerability, confusion, lack of control, feeling unwanted, embarrassment, shame and childlikeness can be overwhelming. Because we are not immune to being human we must find ways of handling these encounters of the desperate kind.

Those who manage to meet their love needs and are able to handle the occasional failure and damage to their self-esteem seem to have several things in common. The first is that they have inner resources of self-esteem. This means that they have ways of comforting themselves and healing their wounds. They also have found ways of creating external connections for helping them manage their lives.

There are so many skills that are required of us in being able to love without destroying ourselves or others. I guess that is an oxymoron, destructive love. But it is crucial for our wellbeing. Can we love without being addicted to love? Can we be disappointed in love and not resort to addiction in order to handle the hurt?

Handling failure, disappointment and pain places the burden on us to comfort and heal ourselves. In my experience addiction prone people often have a great deal of difficulty in this area because they have been deeply wounded.

In order for healing to take place means we must address both the old wounds as well as finding ways of coping with the overwhelming feelings that often go with disappointment in love. One client admitted to me one day, "Doc, I don't know the first thing about how to love someone. I have never had it and I screw up all of my relationships."

Restoring self-esteem and learning to love ourselves always needs a quality recovery network of loving and supportive relationships. Self-esteem always needs a context. We do not become human in isolation. Too often people focus on self-esteem as an internal problem. They focus on being strong, independent and not needing others. Empowerment is the buzz word these days. We must fight the demon of "co-dependency." In fact, most people prefer to focus on themselves. It is less complicated and that way they avoid the whole confusing and complicated world of relationships. There is less vulnerability in isolation. Co-dependency, however, also has its well documented hazards. It seems then, that love has a price no matter which way we turn. We can be dependent and lose our identity, isolate and be alienated or we can love and be hurt. What price love? The solution? There isn't one. One, that is, which is free from pain or risk. That is the drama of being human. It is unfolding all around us every day. All of life is about trying to love and be loved. Every thing else is a masquerade.

Self-esteem needs nurturance, it needs quality connections and meaningful attachments. Love needs a cradle, a cocoon to help it grow. We also need inner resources to create and carry out the self-esteem project for ourselves. Finally, what we care about and the quality of our attachments defines us. I become what I love. The impoverished life, the unlived life, and the life of quiet desperation all come from the same root: the failure to love. Addiction and addictive love also come from the same root.

**NOTES**

# 4

# **RELATIONSHIPS**

The essence of relationships—togetherness, separateness and loving nurturance, are the foundation of human identity. We exist in relationships and it is the quality of our relationships which determines our ability to actualize our individuality. Individuality and relationships are the tension which drives the engine of human experience. For it is in precisely the dynamic ambivalence of relationships that we experience our greatest fears, deepest needs, most private agonies, greatest confusion and ultimate fulfillment. Being known, accepted, understood, and affirmed for our very selves becomes the basis, the foundation of our own self-knowledge, understanding, acceptance, **self-affirmation**, and ultimately self-actualization. We actualize the imago through relationships.

In the previous segments we have discussed the importance of relationships to self-esteem. It is impossible to discuss human problems and development without having a look at the context in which all of this occurs. We are at every moment in relationship. Relationship is the very nature of being. Whether it is physical, social, interpersonal or to our self, a relationship is our very way of being in the world. It is the quality and characteristics of our being in the world which defines us: our ***modus operandi***. Hence, who we are comes to be defined by our relational style. With this in mind, let us examine more closely some of those qualities of relationships which are so defining.

We will begin by looking at how the poet Kahlil Gibran expressed his view of love and relationships. Sometimes poetry expresses more richly the complexities and nuances of the heart than all of the psychology textbooks combined.

*Then Almitra spoke again and said,*
*And what of marriage, Master?*
*And he answered her saying:*
*You were born together, and together*
*you shall be forever more.*
*You shall be—together when the*
*white wings of death scatter your days and*
*you shall be together in the*
*Silent memory of God.*
*But let there be space in your*
*togetherness.*
*And let the winds of heaven*
*dance between you.*
*Love one another, but make not*
*a bond of love.*
*Let it be rather a moving sea*
*between the shores of your souls.*
*Fill each other's cups*
*but drink not from one cup*
*Give one another of your bread*
*but eat not from the same loaf.*
*Sing and dance together and be*
*joyous, but let each of you be alone*

> *Even as the strings of the lute are alone*
> *even though they quiver with the same music*
> *Give your hearts but not*
> *into each other's keeping*
> *For only the hand of life can contain*
> *your hearts*
> *And stand together yet not*
> *too near together.*
> *For the pillars of the temple stand apart*
> *And the oak tree and the cypress*
> *grow not in each others shadow.*
>
> —Kahlil Gibran
> THE PROPHET

Gibran illuminates the essential paradox of our being together. He suggests that there be space in our togetherness. How to be separate is one of the more difficult aspects of relationships. This is one of those chicken-or-egg quandaries. Which comes first, togetherness or separateness? Can you have one without the other? I believe separateness is essential to the success of any relationship. But the ability to be separate is dependent upon our having had good experiences with togetherness. Separateness is the ability to stand alone, to be self-dependent. In psychological terms, we call this *Individuation*. Individuation is the process by which a child becomes aware of being a self that is separate from others and has developed the ability to be self-sufficient. An individual with self-identity has an adequate self-image, positive self-esteem, clear boundaries, is competent in managing the affairs of life, and is self-nurturing. All of these ideas express the qualities of being separate as a person. Being separate does not mean not needing anyone or not caring about others as so many people seem to think. ***Individuation is not selfishness!***

Being able to function autonomously in the world as an individual also means having the same kind of competence in relationships. The two are inter-dependent. Being intimate with another person implies closeness without losing one's self-boundaries (identity) and not needing to take over the other person's identity (fusion). Many people mistake the feeling of merging with another or fusing their ego with someone else's with closeness. This is the problem of co-dependency. Co-dependency is the opposite of individuation. People who need to feel fused with another or need to rescue or somehow make a career of feeling responsible for others have not individuated. In order to function independently in relationships, one must have secure boundaries and trust: trust in oneself and trust in the other. ***Trust is the cornerstone of all relationships!***

Separateness implies the ability to stand alone—to tolerate both intimacy and distance, simultaneously. It means tolerating your partner's dependency and independence, as well as your own. Being comfortable with neediness in yourself and others suggests that you are capable of self-nurturance. You feed each other but not from the same loaf. This suggests the ability to give from within, that you are bringing something to the relationship and that you are not feeding off each other in a symbiotic or parasitic way.

Lack of individuation presents itself in many ways. People who have difficulty in this area usually are low in self-esteem, are passive and dependent, fear being alone, lack self-confidence, are fearfully jealous, have difficulty expressing anger, exhibit strong desires to control the other, and compulsively seek to please others. This constellation of problems often lead to victimization or abuse in relationships. One cannot be intimate if one has never learned to be separate.

Intimacy is defined as the experience of closeness. Mutuality and openness are created by two persons who are strong enough to be vulnerable and trusting enough to be authentic. In short, who are whole enough to love and be loved without needing the other to make them whole.

The impact of unresolved dependency problems (failure to individuate) on a relationship is considerable. When a person who feels incomplete in their own personhood gets into a relationship they unconsciously are looking for completion. This hidden agenda has to do with the expectation that "When I find someone to love me and take care of me, then I will be okay." The expectation is that the other person is supposed to take care of me, make me feel good, make me feel like a real person and through identification with them feel like I am somebody. I often use the analogy of a person running around trying to find another person they can plug their umbilical cord into. These unconscious expectations frequently end in disappointment and disillusionment. The old refrain, "I don't know what happened. He/she changed. We stopped loving each other, we grew away from each other, etc."

reflects the outcome of this process. The deterioration and distance come about because of lack communication and unresolved conflict.

The need for love is normal, the need for intimacy is normal, wanting to be with someone is normal. Seeking gratification of our dependency needs under the guise of love is where the problem arises. In being together, trying to get our needs met and meeting the other person's needs as well, requires a high level of self-esteem.

**NOTES**

# Meditation

# 1

He walked into my office, turned around and gestured to a woman standing standing behind him and said to me, "I'd like you to meet my self-esteem." I was taken aback, I hadn't heard such a blatant revelation said in quite that way before. There it was, the naked truth hanging in the air right between the three of us. We, needless to say have been working on the problem ever since.

For him, it is a case of being empty with little self-esteem. And for her, she is tired of the burden of being his everything. Having his self-esteem embodied in the form of his recently acquired wife is very problematic for John. For some strange reason things have been going downhill since they married 8 months ago. "I don't understand it Doc, I love her to death, but we fight all the time. I've never been so miserable."

Here, once again, we have the mysterious dynamic of love which has become torturous to its practitioners. We fall in love and feel that particular euphoria that only the elixir of love can provide. We feel wonderful, the world looks great and the other person is magical, they can do no wrong. We feel so alive and whole. So what's the problem. Why so much anger and misery from two people who love each other to death?

As we got acquainted and he told me his story it began to make sense, as it usually does. It always seems abundantly clear once you find out how it came to be. Alcoholic parents on both sides of his family and alcoholic aunts and uncles fill out the family tree. Abuse, both physical and emotional from a very early age coupled with social instability and economic hardship characterized his often chaotic family life.

The effects of this kind of abuse early in a child's life are enormous. The legacy is well documented. Typically these people have tremendous needs for love and at the same time have a great deal of difficulty in trusting and feeling love.

It is not hard to understand that people who have only known abuse don't know how to love and have self-esteem problems. It is only natural to look for love and think that finding someone to love would be the solution. It is: Love is the answer. Then again, what is the problem that love is the answer to? I need love, you need love, the whole world needs love. So I find someone to love me, we meet, we live happily ever after. Isn't that the formula expressed in books, movies, and love songs? In the words of one contemporary song, "I need you to be me, I can't breathe without you."

His wife also, as might be expected, is wounded. Her father was also an alcoholic and was abusive to both her and her mother. He complicated the plot by committing suicide. She confessed to me that what was most frightening to her was seeing her marriage turning into a reenactment of her parents relationship. A serious case of *deja vu*.

She felt responsible for her father's suicide. She felt guilty, as if she might have been able to control his drinking or prevent his suicide.by being more responsible. Her role in the family from a very early age was to try and make the world okay for her parents. Again, this is a normal thing for a child to want to do. We want to please our parents and make them happy, that's what our self-esteem is initially based on. It only becomes a problem when the parents are incapable of providing the necessary conditions for nurturing psychological development. So she needs love, has found someone to love and wants to make him happy, how does all of this go wrong? What causes the dream and fantasy to turn into a nightmare? What causes it to go so haywire that they both want a divorce. What is so wrong that they wound themselves, each other, and act self-destructively?

There are several problems which are not unique to just these two individuals. We all partake of this life mystery; turning love into a living house of horrors. Let's start with the most basic problem first. My client's low self-esteem. He doesn't feel good about himself and doesn't have the first clue about how to make himself feel good. He only knows what he was taught. Once again, if you grow up in a dysfunctional environment you learn how to be dysfunctional. The key to understanding this process is becoming aware of what was learned and seeing that it does not work. The next step is learning new ways of doing things which obtain the desired results. In other words, learn appropriate skills for living and loving.

As a child he learned by trial and error that he felt more in control and competent when he worked and made money. As an adult this became the foundation for his self=esteem. She learned to take care of others and make them feel good. When you put these two together it is apparent that they do not have the kinds of skills which promote intimacy and nurture a long term relationship. Many women have learned that men who are successful in the business world often do not have the skills necessary for success in interpersonal relationships. They are not the same skills.

The basic skills for satisfying relationships are respect, caring, warmth, compassion, communication, understanding, empathy, and responsibility. These skills are not practiced or learned in chaotic and abusive families. In order to have a satisfactory relationship it must be built on a foundation of trust. In order for this to happen I have to know that I am trustworthy and that I can trust you. We do not permit ourselves to be vulnerable or intimate with anyone with whom we fear or do not feel safe. There is risk in being close and experiencing the natural dependence and loss of control that goes with sharing and mutuality.

Fear, anger, ambivalence, jealousy, and conflicting needs are the ordinary stuff of living together. It is the grist of intimacy. Without our shared experience and separateness there can be no passion. What we need are the skills to communicate, listen, care, and respect the other's individuality while preserving our own.

**NOTES**

# Meditation

# 2

Have you ever been in a relationship where, suddenly, you felt trapped, suffocated and imprisoned: so much so that you felt that if you didn't get out of there immediately, you were going to die? I have and probably most of us have felt that way at one time or another. There is nothing quite like this feeling of being alone and yet trapped in a relationship. This week brought these feelings into focus for me when three different people all said essentially the same thing to me. All were in long term relationships of fifteen years or more. They felt emotionally dead and like they had lost essential parts of themselves.

Having been in a twenty year marriage myself, as well as having dealt with these feelings with many clients, it seemed timely to explore them to see what they might teach us about self-esteem. As always we will start with what the feelings are trying to tell us. The feelings are the messenger; they will tell us what we need to know. The first observation is that the feeling of deadness comes from turning off our feelings. People who feel dead are repressors. This is their primary way of dealing with feelings. Feelings which are not dealt with on a daily basis in relationships become ignored, stuffed, repressed or disconnected. On a long term basis this leads to depression, emotional deadness and apathy. This leads not only to a death of our spirit but also that of the relationship.

People who repress their feelings have two qualities in common: they are nice and they are passive. Being nice and passive leads to avoidance of conflict and accommodating to other people's needs. Emotional deadness usually signals that our basic self-esteem needs are not being met. It is like emotional bankruptcy. Beneath all the apathy is a lot of buried hurt, resentment and disappointment. Passive people often feel deeply hurt that their partner has not met their needs. There is an expectation that their partner should take care of them. The short form of this is "if you loved me you would meet my needs." This kind o magical thinking seems to lead to fantasizing about someone who will "love and cherish me in all of my specialness."

In many cases this leads to predictable results, i.e., being dead leads to impoverished emotional states and a vulnerability that leads to meeting someone. We fall in love with someone new, it just "seems to happen." This of course, is the formula for an affair. Or you may handle these feelings by turning to the children for nurturance, or work, or addiction. Usually we turn to an arena where we can feel "special"; where our needs to feel important and worthwhile are fulfilled.

It seems to me that all of this hinges on being able to meet our emotional needs whil eat the same time being in a long term relationship. Elementary isn't it? The key is knowing how and doing it so that the result is we feel more alive and gratified in loving.

In order for this to happen we must break through our own denial and recognize the warning signs of disaster. We must also recognize our own dependency and stop expecting others to automatically meet our needs. One client, a woman put it this way, "I walked into the living room and saw my husband sitting and watching a football game and I felt an overwhelming combination of sadness, rage, despair, suffocation and imprisonment. I just knew that if I didn't do something quickly, or get get out of there, I would die."

The question of interest is why would a woman who has been married for fifteen years suddenly feel all of these feelings in one moment on a nice, sunny, Sunday afternoon. This day was no different than any other, what changed? Simply put, her saturation point had been reached and her ability to repress was overwhelmed. All the feelings she had denied over the years came to the surface at one time. She felt she had to flee. What she really meant was, "I'd better get out of here before I kill him or me."

This particular person did leave. She went for a walk and took a long look at herself. She has been in therapy for a while so she had enough awareness to look at what she was experiencing. Here's what she saw. She saw that she had done this to herself. She saw that she had allowed her husband and her daughter to always be first in getting taken care of. She recognized she had become very angry over the years and blamed her husband for her imprisonment. He was guilty of not being as devoted to meeting her needs as she was to his. She also realized she had not let him know the depth of her disappointment and hurt. And finally she saw that much of this came from her self-esteem problems; her feelings of unworthiness. "The only time I feel important is when I am making some one else happy." I recognize I am deeply afraid of not pleasing him.

After this discussion she went to him and asked him to go for a long walk, She told him to listen and not try to solve the problem. She then told him exactly how she had been feeling and why. She owned the problem and did not blame him. The next time we met her feelings had changed. Her mood of despair had been replaced by optimism. She felt more powerful and in control. After she cleared away her anger she perceived him in a different light.

It is really quite amazing how the dynamics of a relationship can change when we take responsibility for our own happiness. When we stop being so damned nice. Everything changes when we tell them how we feel and teach them how we want to be treated. That moment when she was telling him about her deepest feelings was the most intimacy they had experienced in a long time.

Exercising our power and exposing our needs and fears can be really difficult. The vulnerability is considerable. It can create stormy encounters and generate conflict. But at least it is not boring. The alternative appears to be death until we part; slow death by degree is all too frequently the norm. Passion and conflict can enrich a relationship and produce a vitality that leads to greater intimacy. In this way we may even break out of our solitary confinement.

**NOTES**

# Meditation
# 3

He had been struggling for months to redeem himself in his wife's eyes. He drank and drove the car with the children in it and got a D.U.I.. She won't forgive him. He pleads, begs, bends over backwards, jumps through hoops, and does everything to try and appease her. She's still angry and no matter what he does it's not enough. He's trying to make amends on her terms. His self-esteem is shredded and he still somehow believes that regaining her love will restore him to wholeness. His entire focus is on her, in one session with her he pleaded for her to tell him exactly what he needed to do; he even had a pen and paper ready to write down exactly what she said. He wanted to make sure he got it right.

We can identify with his predicament. At one time or another we have probably felt like we had to have someone's love in order to be okay. Our self-esteem at that moment was in someone else's hands. We felt powerless, vulnerable, dependent and totally at their mercy.

In a flash of insight during our last session he suddenly realized that he had to be in charge of his own "amends". This moment changed some things for him. Now he feels more in control of his self-esteem. He realizes it is up to him to decide what he needs to restore his own self-respect.

The dependency bind my client felt is a familiar one. In his need for love and out of his own fears and feelings of inadequacy looked for solutions outside himself. Guilt looking for forgiveness. This is a distortion or perversion of a very natural condition. We are born into the human family in a helpless, dependent state. We need loving caretaking in order to develop our full humanity. This is the riddle of co-dependency. I need you, you need me and in this dynamic tension lies the source of both our wounding and healing.

The coercive bind of dependency led him to despise himself, and eventually she felt the same way as well. There is a great deal of anger that builds up in dependent relationships. She resented him because she was tired of having to take care of another child. She wanted him to be a man. She wanted to be taken care of for a change; she wanted the father she never had. In fact, it was uncanny how much he was like her father. An alcoholic who abandoned the family. History repeating itself. Likewise, he resented her control and nagging; her criticism was relentless he was such a disappointment, he never could please her--just like his mother.

And so, two wounded, need-filled people found each other out of all the possible people in the world. They fell in love and magically felt whole and wonderful. Ten years later they are disillusioned, angry, depressed and getting a divorce.

There are numerous reasons for divorce and failed relationships, but in my experience low self-esteem and the trap of dependency are responsible for most. People who have not learned how to love themselves and define their own terms for living find themselves in relationships where they are forever trying to be good enough to be loved. The inevitable result is emptiness, anger, and disappointment. It is not love that has failed. The paradox is elegant. I cannot love myself unless you love me, and I cannot love you unless I love myself. The really delicious thing about this paradox is that both statements are true, though apparently opposite.

Paradox is often the starting point of wisdom. It is like the Zen Master who gives his student a Koan (an apparently unsolvable riddle) to solve. The master knows that enlightenment comes not from a solution or an answer, but rather from contemplating and surrendering to the mystery of living in paradox. The student achieves enlightenment in this discovery.

The way that I have grown by living with this paradox is by recognizing that while it is true that my most redemptive moments have come when I was loved for my very self, it is equally true that my ability to live and function and feel good about myself has come when I have felt most alone, unloved and in despair, and was able to draw on my own inner strength. Yet it was because I have had some very important people in my life in the last few years who loved me and taught me to love myself that I was able to step through the doorway of despair and shoulder the burden of my life, redefine myself and go on. In my solitude I am learning to live on my own terms and take responsibility for my life: in short to love myself. The paradox of life; alone, together; dependent, independent. It is the tension which gives birth to the self.

This tension leads to ambivalence about intimacy. It causes us to vacillate between intimacy and isolation. In feeling alone we long to be with someone and when with someone long to be alone. Gibran the poet phrased it very nicely, "let there be space in you togetherness; feed each other but not from the same loaf..."

The paradox of loving is being able to be separate and define our own terms while also being able to surrender to the requirements of loving another. Your terms, my terms, thus we create a life together grounded in love.

Relationships trigger our greatest needs and greatest fears while yielding the greatest rewards and tragedies. Making amends is essential to restoring love in the relationship. It is based on the ability to forgive and live with yourself on your own terms. This is fundamental to regaining self-esteem. Who knows best what will make you feel good about yourself again? But you must also be sensitive to your partner when you have injured her or him. The mystery is that I have no control over whether or not you forgive me. And this is where the great mystery of love is stretched to its breaking point, when we forgive the other and are forgiven.

**NOTES**

# Meditation

# 4

Saying yes and no in life dramatically affects our self-esteem. The manner in which we do this reflects the kinds of boundaries we have. It takes ego strength to clearly take a position whether it is with someone else or ourselves. When we allow another to violate our space we lose respect for ourselves and grow to resent them. When we fail to say no to ourselves we usually become impulsive and or self-indulgent. Those who say no all the time usually are unhappy, bitter and isolated. Difficulty in being able to say yes and no appropriately is usually reflective of early disturbances in psychological development within a dysfunctional family. In short we did not learn to be appropriately powerful and independent, or that we had rights to be separate as a person.

Saying no and yes at the right time and under the right conditions requires the ability to be separate within a relationship. When we say yes to life it takes courage; it involves taking risks, being vulnerable and open to the possibilities. In saying no, likewise, we must also have the courage of conviction in order to take a stand and oppose someone. Sometimes the hardest person to say no to is oneself.

All of this came to mind as I was working with a woman who is in the midst of separating from a man with several different problems. He is manic-depressive, and attempts to self-regulate (medicate) with alcohol, caffeine, and other drugs in various combinations. That he was out of control is an understatement. In order to take control of her life she felt she had to leave him.

This was difficult for her for a lot of reasons; she still cared for him, they managed to have a good time when he wasn't "crazy", and he was a bright and well educated man with whom she had a lot in common. She had tried for several months to get him into some kind of treatment. He resisted, made promises he didn't keep and periodically blamed it all on her.

Finally, she got to the place where she could not tolerate the situation any longer. She was having to face the issue of defining her own boundaries to herself and to him. In using the term boundaries I am indicating that area where my identity and my sense of self ends and yours begins. For many people boundary issues bring into clear focus the problems in that relationship. As she got further along in the divorce process she found that many of her own problems were crystallizing. She discovered she had a real problem in telling him exactly what she wanted and needed. She was also having a problem in defining clear consequences if her needs weren't met. He on the other hand promised her anything but fulfilled nothing. He said yes but meant no. Most of all, as she struggled, she discovered she was having a hard time saying, "its over."

As she began packing her things to move, her issues surfaced. She realized she was deeply afraid of being alone. She also confronted her own dependency needs. She had married a man who in many ways was a little boy who needed a woman to run his life and care for him; primarily because he never learned how. She learned that she appeared to need someone to take care of; primarily because she also did not now how to care for herself. It is typical that co-dependent people find each other and then have these kinds of boundary problems.

All of this came out one night in a group session. Her need, fear, ambivalence, anger and confusion emerged as Jane confronted her difficulty in saying no to him. He was enticing her back by offering a nice trip to her favorite place so they could work on the relationship. Jane admitted she was considering doing it: "I think I will do it, what could it hurt? we are still good friends and have a great time together." I asked her to look at her motivation for going. She said, "I'm afraid if I say no he might think its over." The group burst spontaneously into laughter. She and they were able to see how absurd her statement was. She was divorcing him, still wanted to be friends and didn't want him to get the idea that just because she was living some place else that it was over. I laughed as well and admitted that what scared me was that I understood this madness.

This is classic. It reflects the intense conflict we feel in our dependency and the conflicting fears and needs which arise in our relationships. We want to be strong, independent and competent free to determine our own destiny. While at the same time we want to be affirmed, loved, cared for and significant to someone else. Jane was very much aware of trying to have the best of both worlds. She was trying to say yes without having to say no.

Fear of being alone, fear of conflict, fear of rejection, fear of anger, all of these come to the surface when we confront boundary issues. Self-esteem and self-respect hang in the balance. Jane was aware that the less she said no to him the less respect she had for herself. The more she said yes to him the more she felt out of control. When she attempted to define herself all of her fears came out. This is a tough place for all of us to be. Most Of the time we arrange our lives so that we aren't aware of the terror that lurks beneath the surface. It only comes into focus in boundary situations: those defining moments when we say yes and no. Paradoxically these are the times when we grow the most or the least. We grow when we face the fear and live on the boundary. Anxiety and despair are the doorway to self-hood. When we retreat from the boundary and refuse to define ourselves we lose something of ourselves. There is power in saying no. There is power in saying yes. But the power to define ourselves comes from saying yes and no at the right time.

**NOTES**

# 5

## Anger

Anger is a powerful force in the lives of people. It contains the energy for self-preservation and great creativity as well as the power to disrupt and destroy. It is present, always present, but often denied and unrecognized. In this portion we will look at anger, its causes and relationship to addiction and self-esteem. Perhaps in the process you will learn to recognize and become aware of anger, decipher its complex messages and find constructive ways to give it expression.

Anger wears many masks. In its undisguised form, it may be seen as full blown rage or an uncontrolled outburst. Anger is one thing in adults, another in an adolescent and still quite a different matter in a child. In its disguised form anger may come out as subtle satire, veiled sarcasm, irritability, substance abuse, or vague hostility. Violence or myriad forms of self-destructive and or anti-social behavior are its more obvious overt expressions. Anger's many forms of expression range in intensity from mild to extreme and in appropriateness from the socially acceptable to blatantly destructive. Our first experience of anger usually begins within the family. It is in the commerce of every day living that children come to learn about anger's many complexities. Our experience of anger in this context will determine, to a significant degree, how comfortable we are with our anger as well as the anger of others. How well anger is handled in relationships, whether interpersonal or international determines, to a large extent, the success or failure of those relationships. Most societies have rituals and rules for managing conflict and redressing personal injury. War is one of those ritualized modes of aggression that governs international aggression.

Anger is a universal human experience. Everyone gets angry. It is as basic as all of the other human emotions we have been discussing. The problem with anger is that it is so threatening that some people have difficulty in recognizing it in themselves. Or in the opposite extreme, anger is so powerful that it is beyond control. The greater the difficulty in feeling, recognizing and controlling anger, the more difficulty a person will have in meaningful relationships and the greater the likelihood that it will come out in some form that will have negative consequences.

We are born with the capacity for anger. It is necessary for our wellbeing. Anger, like all the other emotions, serves an important function in enabling us to survive in a complex world. The things which make us angry, the ways in which we respond when others are angry, and the particular feelings we have about our own anger are all learned. Our culture has very complex rules pertaining to anger; anger with children from adults; anger between adults who know each other; anger between adults who do not know each other; anger between male and female; the list is endless. These rules get transmitted through parents, peers, school, government and the mass media.

Not all the rules about anger are necessarily helpful or

even make sense. This is particularly true if one grew up in a dysfunctional family. In this kind of family the emotional climate may be far too controlled, or even entirely absent of feelings; in others, there may be too much of one kind of feeling and not enough of another.

What is characteristic of dysfunctional families is that not all feelings are permitted and feelings are judged as good or bad. In healthier families emotional output is consistent and appropriate. In this atmosphere, children know how their parents feel and why. It is especially easy to know when a parent is angry. This is because feelings—all kinds—are accepted. And what is most important is the child learns a feeling of comfort and safety from the expression of these feelings. People feel angry, or sad, glad, hurt, depressed, or tenderly loving. No one gets hurt, no one hurts themselves. People in this climate are what they feel; and it is acceptable. In this climate a child picks up the tone of consistency, openness, and warm acceptance regarding all feelings. The child learns: "I am loved and accepted; I am safe with my feelings; I don't need to stifle or pretend to please you." "I and all my feelings are welcomed in this family, I belong." And because my feelings are accepted, I learn that I am worthy and acceptable. Anger, then, is part and parcel of the ongoingness of people living together.

For many people, however, the emotional climate of their homes was not like this. So many have grown up afraid to feel, afraid to express feelings and afraid to be around others who feel and express their feelings. This is particularly true of anger.

In my particular family anger was strictly taboo. I learned that nice boys did not get angry. This taboo stemmed from a family that was cold and devoid of emotions. I never saw anyone express sadness, joy, or anger. The only anger, and it was destructive, was expressed by my father who ridiculed and demeaned my brother and myself for being weak, needy or tearful. What was communicated by this behavior was "don't feel, don't expose any weakness, and don't need; it is not safe to expose anything of yourself." The net effect is to deaden all feelings.

I remember being angry as a child, I had a very quick temper but soon learned to keep it hidden. The anger toward my father was suppressed: too dangerous to show. I became fearfully over-compliant. Occasionally I would "accidentally forget" to do something my father wanted me to do, or I would do something which drove him nuts. I was constantly getting my shoes wet. This, for some reason, drove him crazy, but how could he be mad at me? "I just forgot, or it was an accident." I was learning a process of denial, of not taking responsibility for my anger, and how to passively and indirectly act out my rage at him. **Take a moment here to write about how you express your anger. Feel free to explore the rules for anger in your family. Do not judge yourself for your feelings.**

Anger which is not owned, felt, or expressed will be manifested somehow. It may turn inward in the form of guilty self-criticism or it may become totally repressed and thus experienced psychosomatically. These somatic expressions can take many forms. Headaches, ulcers, muscle tension, spastic colon, high blood pressure and allergic reactions are all common anger related disorders. It may also come out indirectly in other kinds of emotional reactions such as hostility, depression, anxiety, guilt, pouting, sullenness, irritability, and sudden rage. And more particularly, anger may be at the root of substance use. It is very common for individuals to go out and drink every time they get emotionally upset and angry. Still even more common is the tendency to express anger after having a few drinks, and then later deny the anger. "It was the booze that was talking." Certainly, the studies are clear on the relationship between drug and alcohol abuse and family violence. Anger and mind altering chemicals are a volatile and dangerous mixture.

There are many strategies for dealing with anger, both our own and others. One defense against anger is *projection*. By attributing anger to others, it is safely disowned. As if to say this isn't my anger, everybody else is angry. Another is *displacement*. Kicking the dog is a classic example of displacing anger from the real target which may be dangerous to a target which is not as likely to retaliate. *Scapegoating* is another form of dealing with aggression indirectly. This is more often found in groups. Again, it is a means of dealing with anger which is felt within the group and taken out on a target outside the group. This defuses inner group tension and acts as a safety valve for feelings. These are just a few of the more common defenses found in dealing with anger and aggression. Though these defenses partially work to handle anger, they often do not get to the causes. Even more importantly, anger which is not handled constructively does not go away, it becomes an extremely contaminating, hidden force in all relationships.

The roots of anger are probably as numerous as there are people. However, there are several common causes which seem to transcend various cultures. Basically, anger is an innate biological and psychological reaction to threat, frustration or injury. It is part of the protective, defensive system which provides sufficient arousal to fight or problem solve. The modes of expression or non-expression as the case may be, are a product of learning and social convention.

In relationships where anger can be very threatening, it seems to arise out of dependency and interdependency conflicts. Most relationships have an instrumental function in that they are established to meet certain needs. These needs vary from economic to recreational to affectional. What is crucial to the welfare of these relationships is the degree to which conflict is managed. Anger is the byproduct of unmet needs and disappointed expectations. Hostility occurs because first of all, expectations are unclear to the person who has them, and secondly, they are not expressed to the partner. This leads to frustration, distance, retaliation and further complications.

In essence, anger is a complex emotion, which if it is not dealt with, can become a toxic force. A toxin which poisons the body, disrupts relationships, and results in many perverse psychological reactions.

Anger is complex because it has many sources. It may result from unmet psychological and physical needs, as well as stemming from beliefs, self-talk and expectations. It is paramount for our total wellbeing that we deal with our anger. The more that anger can be recognized, understood, and given direct expression the healthier we will all be.

Some signs of withheld anger include: an increase in anxiety, depression, and phobias. An increase in obsessive thinking, disturbances in sleep, and an increase in numerous self-destructive behaviors such as drinking, spending, eating or sexual escapades. At the somatic level, unexpressed anger may result in headaches, ulcers, spastic colon, high blood pressure, neck and back spasms, and chest pains. Clearly, an emotion this powerful needs great awareness and skill in expression.

**NOTES**

# Meditation
## 1

Anger and self-esteem are deeply connected in much the same way that Old Faithful is related to underground geological forces. Anger is indicative of the status of our self-esteem venture. When we experience anger it is a signal that in some way our need to preserve and enhance our self-esteem is being thwarted. Anger for most people is a difficult emotion. When not handled well, it can lead to many social, interpersonal and personal difficulties. I have found that anger is a powerful factor in addiction and unsuccessful recovery. There is a complex relationship between anger, self-esteem, and addiction,

Anger is a primary emotion; it is present from birth. How we experience it and how we express it are matters of temperament and training. I believe the connection between anger and self-esteem lies in our primary motivation to establish, preserve and enhance self-esteem. If this is true. then anger is a marker of the success of this venture.

Notice how you respond when your self-esteem is on the line! Most people become defensive. Our biological response is to either fight or flee. Beyond this initial response, everything else is a matter of learning and of context and the result of what is going on in our heads.

Anger is a normal, natural, inborn response. Many of us have been taught that we shouldn't ever become angry. This has led to a taboo on anger. When this happens we usually suppress our anger or turn it off to the point of not even being aware of how we are feeling. Most of us have problems with anger in one or more of three areas: 1) recognizing it, 2) feeling it, 3) expressing it.

I have a client, a middle aged man, who recently came in with his wife after having spent a week in the hospital for medical testing. He exploded in frustration. "They didn't find anything wrong and didn't do a thing for me!" He then proceeded to spend the entire session ventilating his anger at his job, his wife, his teenage son and at me. After listening to his tirade I tried to calmly ask him if perhaps there might be a connection between his anger and the irritable bowel syndrome that had caused him to be hospitalized. He responded by trying to convince me that there was nothing wrong with him. It was his wife, his boss, his son, blame, blame. If I could fix all of those people, he implied, he would be just fine.

Though he had little difficulty in admitting he was angry, it was clear that he had little insight into how he was participating in his own pain. He was totally disconnected from his anger.

As he told his story, it became apparent that he felt victimized. He himself was helpless in the face of all these problems. It was eating him up inside. His self-esteem was on the line in every instance. Because of the way he handles his anger, he alienates everyone around him. Who wants to be close to someone who is demeaning, angry, hostile, blaming and continually complaining?

If this person were an addict he would drink or fix every time his frustration and anger reached intolerable levels. His anger is so toxic that it is affecting his body and may cost him his health. It could also cost him his job and family.

What can be done about this? Recovery, or change, begins with recognizing and examining the problem. In this case, anger is serving a very important function. As with all feelings, it is serving as a messenger.

The first step is to listen to and then decode the message of anger. Since our feelings are entirely subjective, it is important to understand our own anger. If you find anger predominating your moods and poisoning your relationships, it is time to examine the feeling and to understand where your anger is coming from. But how do you do that?

I recommend sitting down and writing the autobiography of your anger. Start with the feeling and explore it. Usually it will take you back to the source. This will pinpoint the problem and help you assess the difficulty. It may take a lot of time and could involve healing old wounds and coming to grips with past pain, Anger often masks unresolved hurts and untended injuries.

Finally, once you have identified the anger and learned all you can about it, the next step is to learn more constructive ways of expressing it. This will put you back on the road to recovery of your self-esteem.

Anger is not the kind of emotion which can be ignored. If, like my client, you fail to deal with it, it can become a huge, toxic force that could poison you in body, mind and spirit and significant relationships.

# Meditation

## 2

"My energy is coming back and it is scaring me. I had a dream in which a Green Monster with razor sharp teeth was eating me alive." My client, a middle aged alcoholic, divorced, minister was beginning to discover that his anger had many faces. In this discovery he was seeing how in its unrecognized forms anger had ruined his marriage, career and almost his life. The discovery was bringing him out of a deep depression he had been in since he stopped drinking 18 months ago. Experiencing his anger was causing him a great deal of fear. "I am a monster because of my anger," he said. "I am so afraid that I could hurt my kids, or my wife, or even myself," he confessed.

His anger had manifested itself in many disguised ways over the years. He is recognizing that he drank because he was angry at his wife. He never stood up to her directly. He spent money impulsively for trinkets he didn't need. This drove his wife crazy because of his "irresponsibility". We call this disguised anger passive aggression. He didn't finish his doctoral dissertation and procrastinated his way out of graduate school because he resented the demands of his professors. He drank when he felt the expectations of his congregation were too great. And he experienced headaches, upset stomach, and back pain when his mother would try to control his life. All of these are common symptoms of unrecognized anger.

Anger has many faces, some are very easy to recognize

particularly when they are in the overt forms of violence and naked aggression. It is not so easy to recognize when it comes in indirect ways such as procrastination, psychosomatic illness, impulsive behavior, depression, guilt, and compulsions. The list of indirect modes expression is probably endless.

Unrecognized anger has destructive consequences to self-esteem because it often results in self-destructive behavior. It of course, has devastating effects on relationships when not handled appropriately. Abuse, family violence, and chronic conflict are the more obvious symptoms of interpersonal anger which is allowed to go unresolved.

Why is anger such a big deal? Why does it take such devious and monstrous forms? And what can be done to unmask and defang it? These are critical questions anyone in recovery must eventually face.

First of all, anger is only a big deal if we make it into one. Anger is a naturally occurring emotion just like all of our other emotions. It occurs usually under conditions of threat or frustration. It is part of our emotional brain's defense system. If we are threatened our body responds by either preparing us to fight or flee. What is determinative is the psychological spin we put on the event (interpretation). The psychological significance we attach to what happens to us is a function of previous learning and current context. In short we deal with anger the way we were taught by our family and society.

My client's experience of anger as a child was not helpful. He was taught that he was "bad" when he was angry. His anger was met with shame and guilt from his mother and episodic rages from his father. In essence he learned to repress all anger: to direct it against himself if he felt it, or express it violently when it built up. Drinking became a way of anesthetizing his anger and relieving the stress of so much tension. This attitude toward anger is not uncommon, particularly in "Evangelical Christian" homes. My family background is similar. I learned anger is bad; my mother taught me to be stoic and my father demeaned and ridiculed me with his anger. I learned that anger was never dealt with directly.

Under these conditions there is nowhere to go with anger except underground. Since conditions which create anger don't go away, the anger must go somewhere. This is how anger takes on its more sinister guises. Unrecognized and unexpressed anger potentially can become monstrous. There are many reasons why anger is not expressed directly. Some people have become fight or conflict phobic. I have a client who is so afraid of conflict that she lets everyone take advantage of her. She got a divorce and never asked for alimony or child support because she didn't want to make her husband angry. What was he going to do, divorce her? Others are afraid of abandonment or have a need to be loved and feel that if they get angry they will lose their source of self-esteem (co-dependency). Others have been raised in chaotic, violent and abusive homes and have been thusly traumatized by anger.

The first step in anger management is *Awareness*. At some level we must become conscious of anger as a problem either for ourselves or for others. A lot of Step work in this area can be done with doing inventories, talking with sponsors and getting feedback with others on how to handle anger. Keeping an *Anger Diary* is another way of getting in touch with and tracking anger. If you have difficulty in even recognizing or experiencing anger then you need to work on getting touch with your body. Anger always has a bodily expression. I call body work "an organ recital" Essentially this means to pay attention to your body. Listen to your stomach, your neck, your tension, pain, etc. Ask yourself if these symptoms could be unexpressed anger. The symptom is the messenger. If we kill the messenger we lose the critical opportunity to learn what is making us angry.

Once we have learned to identify the feeling we are ready for the next step: **Assessment**. This entails learning about our anger. Learn what causes it. Learn how it has affected your life. And learn the dysfunctional ways you have been using it to sabotage yourself. Learn how you use anger to control and manipulate others. Finally, learn more appropriate, adaptive, ways of expressing it. This is the final stage in leaning to defang the monster: **Action**.

We need to continually bring anger into our conscious awareness. This will lead to acceptance of these feelings as normal and necessary. Bringing anger out of the closet into the family circle by unmasking it will make it far less threatening and destructive. Learning to express anger appropriately will energize and empower you. In relationships that have become dull, stagnant and boring, anger may revitalize passion and intimacy. You can't be intimate if you can't be angry.

You also can't be whole if you can't be angry. Unrecognized anger may be the roadblock to your recovery. When we confront the monster we take one more step toward reclaiming our lost power and self-esteem. Like most things, the monster once discovered and faced takes on a striking resemblance to the face in the mirror.

# Meditation

# 3

"Sometimes I feel so mean-spirited, I don't like myself, I don't like other people, I don't like life." I was asked to comment on these feelings the other day as they might relate to the topic of self-esteem. As I began organizing my thoughts, a number of approaches came to mind. I could write about "forgiveness," or "acceptance," or "anger"; they all seem to be related to this feeling. And I might add, they are critical to self-esteem. I also seem to recall that I have written on each subject at one time or another. Yet, I continued to resonate with the feeling. I however, wanted to write about it from different perspective. And then it came to me as it usually does, a phrase from my creative unconscious, that said it just right. When I feel so mean-spirited it is because *I am at war at the core.*

What do I mean? I mean that when I am experiencing this kind of free-floating anger which contaminates everything I am very distressed in the very center of my being. Anger can come from many sources. It can signal that we are frustrated. It can indicate we have some unresolved guilt. It can be a symptom of hurt or fear. And finally, anger is often associated with helplessness or feelings of life dissatisfaction.

Anger is a very complex and important emotion which has many fears and taboos associated with it. For many, anger gets us pretty uncomfortable. It's hard to recognize, understand, and even harder to express appropriately. Anger of the spirit is even more difficult to work with. It is problematic because it is so powerful and because it goes to our soul. This is why I think it is a core issue and is fundamentally based in self-esteem. It is a core issue because this kind of anger reflects a deep-seated conflict within us that has to do with how we are feeling about who we are.

When I am at war at the core I am on the warpath. The world is full of incompetent stupid, inconsiderate, insensitive and inadequate people. The world is a mess, etc.. I was having dinner at my favorite hangout the other night and made the mistake of getting into a conversation with a woman at the counter sitting a few stools away from me. It wasn't a conversation really, it was a 30 minute diatribe--"the world is going to hell in a hand basket .....the kids today.....the politicians.....the schools....etc.. You've probably heard it yourself, maybe even felt that way. She was a volcano of anger, spewing forth her toxic waste over anyone who would listen; she mistook me for someone who was listening.

She was externalizing her anger through projection and expressing her very deeply felt feelings about herself. The world and other people are like a giant movie screen where we portray our inner melodrama.

This kind of anger is noted for its intensity and for it's pervasiveness. I'm sure this wasn't the first time she said those things. With her it is a chronic life-position whose net effect is to turn others off and drive them away. Since I did not want to argue and was not in the position to work with her anger in a meaningful way, I just agreed with her, "ain't it awful," I said. Since she wasn't looking for insight or change and the world was the problem in her eyes I left her to her poisoned position.

Recovery is never easy, and the road to recovery seldom begins on a barstool or at the counter in a restaurant. It usually begins when we tune in to our inner voices and try to hear and understand the message.

The answer to soul anger is reconciliation. We need reconciliation at the core because there is a fundamental rift in the way we feel about ourselves. We are deeply divided because we are rejecting something of ourselves we are ashamed of, afraid of, or because we just don't like that part of ourselves. We fundamentally, are against ourselves. The unconscious, the shadow, the dark side, our evil twin, the devil, however you want to think of this part of yourself needs healing. The more you resist, fight, repress, or run from this part of yourself the more intense it becomes. Just like international wars, they escalate until someone can get all the warring factions to sit down at the peace table.

Finding inner peace and ending the war at the core is similar to the international peace process. Someone needs to be a peacemaker because too many innocent people are suffering. So, declare a truce. Invite the warring parties to sit down at a table. Gather the facts of the dispute. Listen to the grievances. Get to know the issues, what do they really want? You must know them intimately. Guarantee safety and the right to exist to everyone. Let every voice be heard. This is crucial because most of the time the problem is worsened by one side trying to win through destroying the other side. Understanding is only accomplished through true dialogue.

The keys, then, to reconciliation are; (1) listen to the message in the anger or dis-ease, (2) declare a truce, (3) go on a fact finding mission, (4) engage in a dialogue, (5) legitimatize the rights of all, (6) define the problems, and (7) search for solutions. Peace and inner harmony can only come through acceptance, understanding, compassion and dialogue. This is the essence of reconciliation. Let there be peace through love at the core.

**NOTES**

# Meditation

# 4

Preserving and enhancing self-esteem are the defining and motivating forces in human interactions at both the personal and social levels. If this is true, then how and why do people kill themselves or engage in self-destructive behavior?

When we feel competent, significant and experience our lives as meaningful, we have a sense of well-being and fulfillment. Conversely when we feel inadequate, insignificant and that life is meaningless, existence is very difficult. For some, if the meaninglessness persists for very long, suicidal thoughts seem to spontaneously arise.

The way we go about maintaining self-esteem is what defines our personalities. When our way of life--or self--is threatened, we experience a crisis. I came to understand this principle three years ago in a very unforgettable way. It was five o'clock in the morning on a Tuesday. The phone rang. One of my closest friends was calling to tell me that a colleague and mutual friend we had gone to school with had just committed suicide. My shock and bewilderment were total. I responded with some inane comment about not knowing that he had been depressed. As it turned out, I knew very little about my friend "Frank." What irony and paradox: a psychologist had killed himself. It defies logic. Unfortunately it is not all that unusual an occurrence. In fact, just six months later another friend and colleague shot himself while sitting on a beach.

Of course, the big question is why? I had the unique

opportunity to pursue this question through Frank's journals which were graciously provided to me by his wife. At the surface, Frank was a typical American success story. Born and raised in rural America, he dreamed of coming to the big city and practicing psychology. He went to graduate school, married and established a practice in Hollywood. At the time of his death, he was in his 40's and was by all appearances, very successful. His wife had a successful career of her own and had just completed her Master's degree. Together, their income was very significant. He was respected by colleagues and clients alike. He and his wife enjoyed an active social life with close friends. Why suicide?

The paradox of self-esteem! Frank had all of the ingredients of what we commonly regard as "the good life" and yet it was not enough for him. His collapse was internal. Frank hated himself and his life: he was deeply against himself. The more he succeeded, the worse he felt. With all of his knowledge and ability, he was unable to establish a viable life that meant something to him. Somehow, his self-loathing and contempt became so great that he was unable to go on. He could not reconcile his success with his own view of himself. The discrepancy was too great. For him, going into therapy, talking to friends or getting some form of help was apparently too humiliating. This inability to come to grips with his self-hatred ended in suicide. Suicide is by definition self-murder, a very violent and angry thing to do to oneself. The will to live in most cases is so strong that most of us engage in desperate measures in order to preserve life. To deliberately take one's own life must mean that something has gone so wrong that the the urge to death overcomes the will to life.

Suicide, of course, is only one way to respond to negative

self-esteem, or to handle anger directed at ourselves. All of us have our own unique ways of dealing with the problem. Destructive relationships, addiction to drugs and alcohol, workaholism are just a few of the ways we attempt to either avoid the pain or feel good for a moment. The truism here is that inauthentic solutions to self-esteem problems eventually become problems in themselves. And though not conscious or deliberate acts of suicide they, in effect have the same end result.

The obvious question arises, then, that if inauthentic solutions lead to self-destruction, what will lead to healing and an authentic response to our psychological pain.

In my view, pain, anger and disappointment are a part of natural human growth and development. It occurs every time we go through a change. Transformation can occur voluntarily or as a result of trauma or irresponsibility. Our response to threat is critical to our self-esteem. Turning pain and anger into a healing experience requires awareness and intelligence. Our survival is based on the ability learn from experience. Suicidal thoughts and feelings are the clarion call to heed the message—it is telling us something.

To respond adaptively, we must begin with awareness: pay attention to the pain, depression or suffering which always indicates a problem. The next step is assessment—understanding the problem. What is the meaning of my self-loathing and despair? Solutions will flow out of our awareness and assessment of the problem.

But awareness and assessment are not sufficient in themselves. We need to carry the process one step further...to action! What kind of action? Solutions which transform our suffering into a healing crisis must stem from a strategy for change (a recovery program). It must be a strategy which addresses the problem and one which will eventually result in a new, viable and sustainable life-style. The formula for transformation becomes Crisis = Awareness + Assessment + Action = Healing. The formula for self-destruction reads differently: Crisis = Denial + Continuation of Same Behavior + Deterioration = Suicide or Other Early Death.

Crises in self-esteem present challenges and opportunities which, when dealt with, can lead each of us to a genuine, caring relationship with oneself. When this happens, we live inside out. That is, we define the terms for our self-esteem and in so doing, create a life which leads to significance, richness and meaning. All that glitters may not feed the spirit or nurture self-esteem. This is what I learned from my friend Frank.

**NOTES**

# 6

# Depression

Depression is a complex and often paradoxical problem for which many people do not even seek treatment. Often, many people, like my friend Frank, are apparently "successful", have a group of long time friends, apparently successful spouses and marriages and are loved and respected by others. Many have achieved stature in their communities. Depression appears in many ways to all kinds of people. Deeply rooted in the universal human condition, records of melancholy and despair are found in the earliest recorded accounts of man's experience.

Depression affects all ages, races, occupations, and socio-economic classes. Everyone at one time or another has probably felt the numbing, deadening, painful, helpless, sense of hopelessness and despair that comes with a loss or a disappointment. This transitory experience comes with the ups and downs in life; the "slings and arrows of outrageous fortune." No one is immune, however, some people appear to be more vulnerable to depression and loss than others. For these people, depression is not a sometimes occurring, unwelcome visitor. Depression arrives like an unwanted relative who comes to stay a week and moves in and totally takes over the household. This kind of depression can become disabling: a progressively deteriorating problem leading to serious impairment in the ability to carry out the daily affairs of life. A common complaint with this kind of depression is: "I don't know why I feel this way, I have everything, but I just can't seem to shake this feeling of doom and gloom."

For our concerns here we are dealing with a dual problem, depression and substance abuse. I raise this as an issue because in my experience depression is both a serious cause as well as consequence of addiction. When a depressed person drinks or uses it may be to "self-medicate." When a depressed person uses alcohol he/she is adding a chemical depressant to the problem of depression. Certainly, depression is a serious problem after a person gets clean and sober because it is the natural aftermath both physiologically and psychologically of addiction. That is why it is very important to understand depression and its relationship to addiction.

Depression has many masks. Its symptoms are varied in severity as well as forms of expression. Despite its many faces, however, depression does have several symptoms which appear to cluster together into a recognizable syndrome.

The usual or essential features of depression are a loss of pleasure or interest in all or almost all of a person's usual activities. This condition is quite persistent over a period of time, usually three to six months. It is also associated with disturbances in appetite and sleep. In heavy people, appetite increases, and in thin people appetite decreases. It doesn't seem fair, does it? There is also a change in energy, some people feel agitated and others feel lethargic. Also noted are changes in thinking with problems in memory, concentration, and often persistent, morbid and melancholic thoughts of worthlessness and suicide. A feeling of guilt, leading to withdrawal from life is common. A person may experience some, or in extreme cases, all of these signs.

Depression in children and adolescents may be expressed by changes in personality and behavior. School performance usually declines, and relationships with teachers and peers often deteriorate. It is very common for adolescents to "act their depression out" in anti-social, rebellious, or self-destructive activity. In young children depression often manifests itself in fears, nightmares and physical ailments and complaints. There may also be a general regression to previous levels of development, like bed wetting, soiling, or clinging and dependence.

Depression may also disguise itself in features that one would not ordinarily think of as depression: health problems, physical distress, irritability, fears, brooding, worry, panic attacks, phobias and insomnia. One person, for example, was referred to me by a cardiologist because of chest pains, rapid pulse and shortness of breath. She had a complete cardiac workup and nothing physically wrong was found, hence the psychological referral. This is often a difficult referral because the individual has the physical symptoms and may resent the implication that they are "crazy". Once I saw this person and reassured her that the referral didn't mean that her physician thought she was "crazy", together we were able to discover that she had been suffering from depression for years.

In sum, depression is a disorder which may be manifested by disturbances in thought, feeling and behavior. It also affects the physical functioning of the body. In some individuals it affects only one domain, and in others it may involve all.

In order to unravel the complexities of depression in real

life, one must look to the total picture presented by the sufferer. Depression, when looked at in totality, is a signal that is to the psyche what pain is to the body. It is a distress signal indicating that a person is suffering from psychological malnutrition. Just as joy and pleasure are byproducts of pleasurable activities, so, likewise depression is a byproduct of interactions that leave the self feeling depleted, exhausted, numb, helpless and hopeless.

To return for a moment to a previous discussion, depression is a result of an individual's inability to maintain self-esteem. By looking at depression from this perspective, we may see that it stems from the very roots of human personality.

When the needs for competence, significance, and meaning are not met, depression is the inevitable result. This point is well illustrated by the death of my friend. He had a severely abusive father and a mother who was distant and cold. He based his whole life (self-esteem project) on achieving his dream of success. In other people's eyes he had "made it". But the dream did not fill his emptiness. No matter how much he achieved, it was not enough. He was still not pleased with himself. In fact, the more he achieved the more guilty he felt for surpassing his father. The critical, internalized father would not let him enjoy his success. To quell his pain, he used drugs and alcohol. His suicide indicated to me both an internal collapse of his identity as well as a belief that there was nothing he could do to make any difference.

This, of course, became a solution that turned into another way to feel bad. This worsened his feelings of self-contempt and guilt. Finally, the body began to break down under the stress and abuse. He became ill from a virus. Emotionally depleted and physically ill, the internal struggle to appear normal became too great. His collapsing world went unnoticed by wife and friends. Seeking help would have been too great an admission of defeat to his self-esteem. He chose what he felt was his final and only option: suicide!

Current stress, vulnerability, low self-esteem, and old unhealed wounds did him in. The need to feel powerful, to be loved, to love ourselves, and to feel that our lives mean something are the most powerful of human needs. Deprived of these, few of us would feel like continuing to struggle. When they are not fulfilled and the possibility of meeting them appears futile, depression is the necessary consequence. When depression signals the failure of the self project, it is imperative that the message is heeded. Depression signals a need for a remedy.

# Meditation

## 1

"I feel depressed... empty... for no reason... I shouldn't feel this way.. I'm so mad at myself. I should be happy. I should, I should, I should, I..."

She finally stopped her torrent of shoulds. I suggested she was really shoulding all over herself. Once she stopped her flurry of beating up on herself for being depressed and unhappy, she could then feel the feelings and begin tracking them. Mary is a middle aged woman who "has no reason to be unhappy"; successful in her career with a "brilliant, handsome husband" a loving daughter and on and on.

She began again, this time reporting that she had had a birthday the previous week and it was Valentine's Day and her husband wasn't very romantic. He is very logical and has to always be right, she said. His birthday present was tickets to go see her favorite musical artist, but he fell asleep during the performance.

As she talked, the clues kept popping up. Birthday, disappointed expectations, she continued telling her story. "I am so unhappy.,. I feel so lonely... I need my husband to appreciate me... I need a soul mate." Her unmet needs continued to pour out.

Depression is such a common experience to us all. Even more common is for people to "be depressed for no reason." In actuality, what happens is that we become aware of our depression, but are not aware of the subtle triggers. In fact, we are rarely depressed for no reason.

In Mary's case, she was experiencing feelings that were troubling and painful and she was doing it sober. Being sober, she was depriving herself of a primary defense against feeling bad and was denying herself a way of feeling better and propping up her self-esteem. Her addiction gave her immediate gratification and was not dependent on her husband.

Depression is an often complicated emotion that has many different, factors which contribute to the experience. My client also revealed that in the previous two years, her mother had died, the Northridge earthquake had destroyed her place of employment and she had moved, losing her group of close women friends. Yet she was upset with herself for being depressed "for no reason". Isn't it amazing that we can be so disconnected and out of touch with ourselves that we are hurting and can't even give ourselves permission to feel bad?

Any one of the following is reason for depression: birthdays, disappointed expectations, marital dissatisfaction, death of a parent, loss of a job we love, a move to another home and the loss of close friends. Clearly, the common ingredient in all of these is loss and the consequence is unresolved grief.

At the root of depression, for my client and perhaps for us all, is self-esteem. She was unhappy and was compounding her unhappiness by shaming herself. Her negative self-talk and self-rejection were both symptomatic of her depression and contributors to it. In addition, because over the past two years she had lost a number of important sources of good feeling and comfort, she had turned to her husband for more support and validation than she normally needed. But he had not risen to the occasion, had not fed her self-esteem as she wanted and "expected". Not surprisingly, her marital satisfaction was diminishing. He hadn't changed: her needs and expectations of him had. Instead of focusing on the positive--his gift of tickets to a concert he knew she would enjoy, even though he didn't care for that particular artist--she focused on the negative--that he fell asleep.

Depression is often symptomatic of unmet self-esteem needs. When we explore the feeling without judgment and permit ourselves to hurt without shaming, it takes our awareness to the next level. But first we must heed the message our feelings tell us about the quality of our lives. Feelings are the byproduct of experience. We wouldn't shame or ridicule ourselves for physical pain, why do we do it for emotional pain? Why do we not accept our feelings as a natural part of life? The answer to this question is simple enough: we were taught not to at an early age by those around us who ridiculed us for feeling.

Mary continued in her exploration of her feelings, going deeper into her pain. "All my life I have not felt understood. I feel like there's something fundamentally wrong with me, like I am flawed at the core." With feelings like these, no one can make her feel loved enough. The soul mate she is looking for is herself. She is like so many of us who look for the solution in others or in something outside of ourselves and always come away disappointed. The illusion is, "If I just had someone to love me, I would be back in paradise again." Spontaneously, my client smiled through her tears and said, "So my homework is to love myself and find some new friends to replace the ones I have lost." She was making progress. As is often the case, when we allow ourselves to feel our feelings the solution to our problem follows close behind.

# Meditation 2

It saddens, fascinates and angers me all at the same time when I encounter a person with a history right out of a textbook. It was as if her parents had read a manual, a classic, on how to be the worst possible parents by destroying their daughter's self-esteem. Parenting by Marquis de Sade.

As she told her story, recounting her difficulties: low self-esteem, poor self-image, depression, loneliness, obesity, and dyslexia, she did it in a stumbling, embarrassed, flat tone. When I asked her about her feelings, she stated she felt numb most of the time. As if to say, "what feelings?" As her story unfolded the symptoms began to make sense, as they always do. How could anyone who has been treated this way not feel the way she does: chronically depressed.

Her father sexually molested her: mother knew about it but indicated that little girls were supposed to please their fathers. Mother called her stupid and lazy while her brothers and sisters demeaned her for being stupid. She soon learned that her role in the family was to serve all of the other members. Sounds like a twisted version of Cinderella, doesn't it? Unfortunately, this fairy tale was a nightmare lived daily by this young woman.

She came to therapy after her mother died and she had recently moved back in to live with her father and brother. "They were going to help her get through her last year of college by letting her stay there." Predictably, her symptoms worsened after she moved back home.

As she discussed herself more extensively she revealed that all of her life she felt stupid, ugly lazy and worthless. The only time she felt "loved" by her family was when they were using her. I suggested now that she was an adult that perhaps she no longer had to put up with their abuse. I indicated humorously, that Lincoln had freed the slaves over a hundred years ago. She looked at me with a puzzled look and said, "I didn't know I had a choice."

Cases like this illustrate for me, so clearly, the nature of self-esteem and the effect that abuse has on the human spirit. We see by the violation of this young woman's psyche the necessary conditions for self-esteem.

First, children must be cherished for themselves. They are not extensions of parental egos. Nor are they for the gratification of adult needs, however perverse. It is the hallmark of dysfunctional families that the children become the means of fulfilling all of the sick parental reeds. Children need to learn that they are worthwhile for who they are, not for what they can do for their parents.

Being cherished and appreciated for ourselves communicates that we are loved and that our existence is uniquely significant. It is in this sense of being valued and respected we come to feel worthwhile. I am somebody to somebody. If this does not occur through normal development it leaves an enormous hunger for love and recognition. When healthy love is lived out daily and is the model for all relationships it becomes a pattern for all future relationships, including the one we have with ourselves. Unfortunately this is also true for unhealthy relationships within families.

The second important condition for self-esteem is autonomy. The course and direction of human development is from dependence to independence. It came as a wholly new idea that she had rights, that she had choices, and that she could have an existence separate from her family. It was a foreign concept because she had not individuated within the family. There were no ego boundaries in this family. She did not learn that everyone in the family is separate and unique with rights to be respected by others.

As part of her therapy I am encouraging her to do some homework. I assigned her the task of writing a declaration of independence. And after that she was to create a personal bill of rights. Independence and rights (boundaries) are signs of emerging self-esteem. We must be free to determine our own identity and be the creator of our own agenda. It is absolutely essential to self-esteem.

A third condition for self-esteem is a sense of mastery or competence. Each of us must experience the joy of being able to do things well. Being criticized and labeled stupid scars the soul. As we can so easily see, this also creates depression.

A final observation about self-esteem has to do with the complex idea of meaning. We all need to live with a sense of meaning, significance and purpose in order to fulfill our potential. Growing up in a dysfunctional family is most disabling because you come to believe that this is normal. Within 'the rules of the family system' we learn the rules for living. We are taught how to behave, what everything means and what is right and wrong. And it is in this context we learn at a most fundamental level who we are. In her case she learned that she was powerless and worthless with no rights. This is the perfect paradigm for learned helplessness, depression, and the self-image of a victim.

When a child grows up and leaves this school for living they find themselves lost in a larger universe where there are different rules. Quite often they find someone who speaks the same language and perhaps went to a similar school. This is how abuse and victimization is perpetuated from generation to generation. That's the bad news. The good news is she has begun to break the cycle. She started the revolution with a simple realization: she has a choice. The second realization was that what she grew up with was not normal. She may spend the rest of her life overcoming the legacy of abuse. But now she is setting the direction of her journey and she is doing it on her terms. She is creating a positive, supportive recovery environment, **a context of meaning and hope,** one which will be a family surrogate. It will help her with the painful process of reconnecting to her lost, split off feelings, healing her wounds, affirming herself and in the process bring herself back to life. Her self-esteem is in her hands now that she realizes she has a choice. As the reader can probably guess, the solution to her poor self-esteem and depression are the same.

**NOTES**

# Meditation

# 3

Many people go along in their lives without connecting the dots. It is extremely common for someone to come into my office and tell me that they are so depressed and they don't know why. And then they tell me in the next few minutes all the things which have occurred that are the explanation but they haven't made the connection. One of the triggers which seem to be "disconnected from consciousness" is the connection between seemingly innocent hurts and the final result: depression. I would like to focus on the relationship between hurt, unexpressed anger and depression. Resentment seems like such a small thing in the beginning, yet it can be as toxic and malignant as cancer. Have you ever wondered why so much time is spent talking about it and why so many people seem to get tripped up in their sobriety by resentment? What's a little anger? Forget it, it's no big deal. Yet the more you repress it, the more your mind keeps turning it over and the emotion keeps coming back. Why?

I don't think it is a problem. It is a symptom. It is a complex reaction that we defend against by minimizing its significance. Resentment is a signal that we have been wounded in our self-esteem. When we experience a blow to our feelings of significance and importance we feel injured and outraged that anyone could do this to us. Resentment usually becomes a problem because we don't go to the person and discuss it with them. A very important factor in resentment is a feeling of coercion and helplessness that goes with the injury. We often feel childlike along with these feelings. And along with this childlike feeling we may also feel the same hurt and sting that we felt as children when we were injured and couldn't defend ourselves.

This childlike feeling is a clue to unraveling the secret of resentment. When we are stuck stewing in our anger with this feeling it typically indicates that something has tapped into some old injuries or wounds that have not healed.

I once had a client who was so preoccupied with an old girlfriend who had hurt him that he could not forgive her. The infantile quality to his obsession came out in the illogical way he looked at it. He blamed her for the injury, yet he was the one who caused the relationship to end because he didn't want to make a commitment to her. In reality he was angry because she didn't love him the way he wanted to be loved. His motto was, "I'll get back at her by suffering--living badly is the best revenge."

This is what children do, they pout and hold their breath to punish mother for frustrating them by not giving in to their demands; right now!

In this example we see rather clearly the dynamics of depression. (1) We hold onto the hurt; (2) we blame the other; (3) we suffer to punish the other so they will feel guilty; (4) the anger is not directly expressed and becomes manipulative and coercive; and (5) the resentment is an expression of a blow to our infantile need to feel special and omnipotent. In short, resentment when not dealt with directly along with the hurt, becomes a festering wound that does not heal. It becomes anger in the guise of depression. Then it spreads to all of our relationships.

Resentment, like all other psychological symptoms is an opportunity, which, when faced, leads to awareness, healing and growth. But first, we must own it as our problem. Acknowledgement of responsibility for our feelings leads to freedom. This is always the first step in problem solving; own it, take responsibility for it. "I am the problem," these are my feelings, "I am not a victim." "You did not do this to me." If we do not take responsibility, then we look at it as the world is being mean to me. This is the victim position; there is nothing I can do to make the world a kinder or more loving place for me, "I am helpless." If I demand that the world worship and bow down before me and pay homage to my specialness I am probably going to be disappointed. By owning the problem I have given myself the opportunity to regain control over things which affect my self-esteem.

Being responsible for ourselves means to assume the burden for our situation, feelings, and behavior. I am the writer, producer, director and star in this little self-esteem melodrama. Change begins with me. Recognition of my feelings and acknowledging their validity leads to awareness. In order to grow we must feel, and this leads to seeing ourselves in action. Letting the buried feelings of hurt and anger surface leads to sometimes amazing results.

Just yesterday I was in session with a woman who has some intense feelings of resentment for her ex-husband. I suggested she write about it. As she did, the whole picture shifted to very deep feelings regarding her mother. My client then stated, "I found myself looking at my ex with a mixture of pity, compassion and acceptance. Now, of course, I have to deal with my mother."

As we feel the resentment, contain it, own it and interrogate it we find the source; old wounds. Healing takes place as we explore the pain and experience wphat is behind the resentment: depression from injured self-esteem and childlike feelings of injury and dependence.

Many times there is nothing that can be done about old wounds in terms of dealing directly with the perpetrator. There may be many reasons for this. Usually, the person is not available or is unwilling to participate with us in the healing adventure. That leaves us with feelings and experiences that are difficult to change.

I find that writing through the feelings and dealing with the complex layers of history leads to resolution of the depression. It has also enabled me to see things from the vantage point of the present. Once I am able to transcend my infantile perspective I am able to see things in an entirely new light.

The key to healing depression is to feel it and discover its many faces. Usually the antidote for depression is taking control and empowering ourselves. When we are depressed we often feel powerless, helpless and hopeless. Any act which restores self-esteem will improve depression.

**NOTES**

# Meditation

## 4

Every once in a while a client puts something into a perspective which for that moment makes everything amazingly clear. This happened in a group last month. It was so clear, in fact, that the group is now using the experience as a way of describing their own experience. This individual's story has become a metaphor for others--a way of seeing and describing life that leads to greater understanding. For this reason I thought I would pass it along.. It has such unique power and clarity.

She is a woman in her middle life: a woman who was profoundly emotionally, physically, and sexually abused by both her father and mother. She is a survivor who inspires us all because of her courage and tenacity. As she told her story she began to describe a problem she didn't know how to handle. Her family moved a lot and each time they moved she had to pack her things into boxes. Her problem? She has all of these boxes from her childhood she has never unpacked. They sit in a warehouse on which she pays a monthly storage fee. Her dilemma is that she can't afford the monthly rent. Someone in the group observed that this is just like life. Isn't it though! It is in fact, a perfect description of the dynamics of depression.

There are several things about this story which are instructive for us on the issue of self-esteem and depression. The first is the idea of putting things in storage. This is a common defense that all of us use to survive painful or unwanted experiences. We repress them and box them away someplace in the deep recesses of our unconscious. Disconnecting and compartmentalizing our lives is a normal defense. It enables us to deal with ongoing reality by setting aside these problems for a time. This strategy is most notable in the case of traumatic stress or chronic abuse. As one can see, the strategy has survival value, but at a cost, usually depression.

Like any defense mechanism when used exclusively it can become a problem in itself. As you can see, she began to compartmentalize her life and acquired a lot of unopened baggage. Like most of us we acquire more and more baggage as we go along. The result is that we have less energy for dealing with present problems. We all pay rent on the past, it is a question of how much. Usually we when we pay rent on the past we end up in emotional bankruptcy with no current operating capital. This is what depression is.

Repressing pain, if used as a lifelong defense leads to emotional deadness. We deaden ourselves and cut ourselves off to prevent more pain. The group in its usual desire to be helpful suggested she just throw everything away or have a garage sale. Herein lies her dilemma. She wants to, but is afraid. She is afraid that sorting through each box will overwhelm her with painful memories. She is also afraid that if she throws it all away she won't "have anything left"

We all have ambivalence about our personal histories. It makes us who we are and yet we can't seem to let it go. It drags us down and prevents us from living in the present. Connecting with the present might bring more pain, while avoiding the past leaves us dead. So we aren't living in the present and we have locked away the past: dead men walking.

So what is the key that will unlock the storehouse and free us from our emotional baggage? Should we run away? Refuse to pay the rent? Burn it down? As I am sure you are all aware, running from our past and our pain only adds to our problems. The real key, as my client is discovering is facing her fear and going into the warehouse a little bit at a time. She began her journey of self-discovery when she joined the group. She took a big step when she made the decision to do something about herself. What is crucial for her is that she is in control of the pace of the journey. She is dealing with it one box at a time. Facing our past and digging around in our psychic storehouse must be done slowly with care, compassion and acceptance. It is difficult to connect with pain, shame, and trauma. It is difficult to face our histories and the wreckage of our past.

Working with our past can be disturbing as well as overwhelming. It is important to not coerce the process. In many ways we have to accomplish the formidable task of learning to feel all over again. It is like awakening from a deep anesthesia. Take one box at a time, one memory will lead to another. Do it in a supportive environment. Do it with a guide or sponsor or someone who has been there. Build bridges to the present which will validate and support your journey.

Know also that there will be some treasures you will want to keep. This was also a factor in my client's search. She knows there are some things she wants to keep. This is also part of the metaphor. Sorting through our histories is painful and involves much grieving but it also grounds us and connects us to ourselves in a very healing way. In the movie "Spitfire Grill", the heroine remarks about her journey, "sometimes healing the wound is more painful than the wound." ***Cleaning house leads to discovering what it is we truly cherish in ourselves and allows us to let the rest go.***

The process seems simple enough. Recognize your problem. Face it. Do the work and you are home free. The problem, of course, is that it is not that simple. Facing ourselves and cleaning out the storehouse is a lifelong process. And then, even if we were to get clear of the wreckage of the past there is still the problem of living well in the present.

Certainly, the benefits of learning to feel again, of gaining awareness and connecting to ourselves as well as others will bring us back to life. Overcoming our ambivalence is a daily challenge to affirm what is worthwhile in ourselves as well as saying yes to life. Growth occurs as we overcome resistance. Doing the work exercises the virtues of compassion, tolerance and acceptance which are necessary skills for living. ***In the process of clearing out the warehouse we are in actuality engaging in the greatest of adventures; the inner journey of self-discovery and healing.***

**NOTES**

# 7

# SHAME AND GUILT

If recovery is ever to be successful, the traveler must navigate the formidable quicksand bog of shame and guilt. This area is one which seems to be the most troublesome. It is probably responsible for more misery, depression, self-destructive behaviors and failed relationships than any other problem. Shame and guilt are the core issue in the development of self-esteem. Let us explore these two very different and separate emotions.

It is very common for most people to group shame and guilt together. They, however, are not the same. They are similar in that they often result in a person's feeling badly about something but are different in their developmental origins. Shame is related to feeling inferior and originates at an earlier developmental period. Guilt has to do with transgression. I have included these two concepts for discussion together because they have to do with autonomy and self-regulation; or in simpler terms, standing on one's own two feet and controlling one's life. Shame and guilt are two of the most common problems which surface in treatment. Often of long standing and deeply rooted origin, shame and guilt cause people to feel very badly about themselves. These lowered feelings of self-esteem are reflected in much self-hatred and self-destructive behavior, and the inability to feel anything at all. They prevent people from loving themselves, or from receiving love from others, and achieving the success and happiness they deserve.

It is important to be able to distinguish between shame and guilt because of the many implications for self-esteem. Most importantly, we must find ways to unburden the self from shame and guilt and thereby be more comfortable in our emotional expression. One cannot move toward the goal of wholeness without unlocking the shackles of shame and guilt.

Basically the antidote for shame and guilt is forgiveness and reconciliation: forgiveness of oneself and reconciliation with others. This requires the development of a more compassionate and understanding way of looking at one's self. As shame and guilt are brought into the light of understanding and the role that shame and guilt have played in distorting relationships is discovered then the person will be able to live with greater freedom. Conversely, the result of unresolved shame and guilt is to have a poor, often hateful relationship with oneself and others. Recovery cannot happen until we become reconciled to ourselves.

Shame, in my view, occurs in human development at an earlier stage than guilt. It occurs concurrently with the emergence of autonomy, which begins at birth and becomes fully an issue by age four. As the self emerges there is a dawning awareness of separateness from others. This consciousness of self begins with the development of language and the growth of the body. As the child begins to experience the power of controlling the bodily functions and acquires mastery over walking, talking, eating, and elimination, he/she is also learning that this emergent independence has an impact on others.

This developmental period is known by most parents as the "terrible two's." The child has learned the power of negation. Saying no means to stand in opposition to others. The child is not only learning to stand on his/her own two feet, literally, but is also learning to stand up to others. In any critical period of human development there is a great deal of vulnerability. The vulnerability at this stage is twofold. What is at risk is the child's sense of self and the tenuous relationship with others.

The child in obeying the biological urges to grow is standing on a crucial bridge to others. How children respond to this new development is important to their self-esteem. The conflict at this stage is between the need for mastery and the need for approval. The child experiences simultaneously the joy of willing, acting, choosing, and freedom with the need to be validated and have significant adults mirror those same feelings of satisfaction and gladness. As if to say, "yes, we too are glad you are growing and are happy for you to become more independent."

If the emerging independence is praised, supported, and nurtured, there is a gain in confidence. If the child is shamed, humiliated or embarrassed, there is an acute lowering of self-esteem. Shame feels like an internal hemorrhage. The child is made aware of being small, helpless, dependent, and somehow defective in character. The shame family of emotions range in severity from shyness, bashfulness, and feeling self-conscious to the more harmful feelings of being demeaned, debased, disgraced and thought of as contemptible. The determinant of course, here, is the strength and quality of the parental reprimand. Criticism may be delivered with tolerance and warmth or with cruelty, hostility and rejection. It is the quality of the response which is important because the parental response with all of its feeling intensity becomes internalized and then becomes a part of the child's reaction patterns.

Being shamed clusters around several basic issues. These issues often have their origin in unresolved parental conflicts over these same issues: *the issues pertain to weakness, incompetence, control, dependency, and perfectionism.*

Criticism or censure from a parent comes as a powerful stimulus to a child. Shame when it enters the relationship cuts like a dual-edged sword. It comes as an immediate sense of inadequacy and at the same time a feeling of loss of that all important affectionate bond with the parent. The net consequence of shame for the child may be formulated as "I have lost your love because there is something wrong with me." This threat of abandonment unleashes very powerful and primitive anxiety. Shame is the feeling of being exposed in all of one's terrible inadequacy; of being unable to hide these apparently unlovable qualities.

Shame can paralyze. It can turn off emotion and prevent the expression of any sense of the self. For the sensitive child it may lead to being chronically apologetic, meek, and excessively approval seeking. In adulthood, shame may be manifested as an inability to carry out and plan any form of independent action. It is also reflected in harsh and punitive self-criticism. Shame is linked to our entire concept of what it is to be lovable as adults. Rooted in these earlier experiences of shame, the adult's independence and self-esteem is undermined.

If shame leads to feeling defective, exposed, vulnerable, and unable to love and be loved. How do we correct it? The solution to this problem must begin with recognition that it is a serious problem. The solution to this problem can be complicated and difficult to resolve because so much damage has been done to the self at such a vulnerable age. But basically, the goal is to regain a sense of validity and legitimacy. To learn to love oneself.

The journey from shame to validity goes through the valley of despair. For the first encounter with shame is often depressing. As we encounter very early and painful memories it can be quite overwhelming. As we search for the love we never got as a child, the despair threatens to engulf. To recognize this painful state as we realistically appraise our parents means we must break through the denial and tendency to idealize them. To work through the pain is to feel the full force of the lovelessness of one's life. It often turns out in this encounter that "I didn't feel loved then, and I have been searching ever since for the love that I missed."

Once the journey has begun with awareness of the problem, transformation may occur when we recognize the shameful ways we treat ourselves. To overcome this problem, a person must do two things. The first is to confront the feeling of being defective. Only you can give yourself the right to be. Secondly, a new relationship with yourself must begin. One that is based on acceptance, understanding, forgiveness, and compassion. In essence, the most difficult task of all is learning to love ourselves in spite of never having been loved. We must teach ourselves how to love. No one can do this for us. We are the problem and the solution. Who can give us a sense of legitimacy and validity but us? All to often we pursue the illusory idea that if I can just find the right person to love me, then I will be okay. This illusion leads to disillusionment because no one can love another person enough to fill the void caused by shame. In fact, shame prevents us from feeling the love we so desperately desire because we feel so unworthy.

In summary, shame is an experience of lost approval that leads to a complex blend of experiences which at the core caused the self to feel devalued and exposed. It originates in the earliest of developmental stages where the child is emerging as a separate human being testing his/her power and autonomy. Shame affects the ability to value the self, to act independently and also the critical interpersonal bridge of shared esteem with others. Shame when it becomes a part of the self's enduring relationship with itself may be triggered by any criticism, disappointment or perceived failure. This is where shame must be identified and confronted. By listening to the language of self-criticism we engage in. We treat ourselves the same way the critical and shaming parents treated us. This must be rooted out. Finally, shame turns the self against itself. It limits self-love and is characterized by perpetual self-contempt. All of this because in our state of being small, dependent, incompetent and defenseless we were ridiculed and demeaned: it is the failure to love at an elemental level.

## Guilt

And now let us turn our attention to the problem of guilt. Getting along in society means being able to meet one's needs while being sensitive to the social situations around one and governing oneself accordingly. This self-governing capability is learned through the socializing influence of family and school. These become the primary social agencies responsible for transmitting society's values. Moral development goes hand in hand with the emotional, social and intellectual development of a child. Development of a conscience is a much more complex process than just learning a set of rules and teaching a child to feel badly when he/she violates them. Moral development includes in its most basic form the ability to discriminate between right and wrong, but it also includes the more complex abilities of perceiving and being sensitive to the needs of others (empathy). It also means being able to establish routines, controlling impulses, and accepting responsibility for personal actions. Learning to discriminate various social roles and how to interact properly with others is also an important aspect. In its most highly developed state, moral development means becoming aware of cooperative and interdependent relationships which are necessary for the greater good of others and society. These are abstract moral principles which often transcend rules and law. For example, Nazi guards who obeyed orders to execute prisoners were acting within the law of their land, but were violating higher moral principles.

Moral development is a complex social learning process which goes through several stages. The experience of guilt also goes through the same process. It is intricately tied to the socialization practices of parents and other adult authority figures. Guilt is the byproduct of moral development. It reflects how the socialization process has become internalized as the quality of the moral sense.

Historically, psychology has treated this development as superego formation. This is a term which is used to describe the socialization process which leads to being capable of self-governing. In essence, the superego is the internalized values of a culture as it finds its expression in an individual conscience. In simple terms, it is easiest to think of conscience as the internal voice of one's parents. The net effect of the superego is that we treat ourselves the way we were treated. In this regard it is important to understand the ways your parents disciplined you, responded to your mistakes, and failures, and misbehavior. Quite often, a great deal of work in therapy is in reworking the superego.

If the quality of the superego is harsh, critical, demeaning, impatient, and judgmental, in short a tyrant, then the task is formidable. Each of us must, finally, if we are to live with any contentment, learn to develop our own values, govern ourselves, and learn to be compassionate with our failings.

Guilt and moral development do not necessarily progress in a smooth line through the developmental stages. They are subject to the same processes of human development as the other matters we have been considering. Guilt and moral development may get stuck at a particular level or become perverse in its manifestation because of the context in which it was learned. When this occurs, the child may have serious problems in self-regulation, knowing appropriate social behavior, aggression, anti-social behavior, or of being unable to engage in cooperative behavior with others.

Those who do not conform to the rules of society are labeled "deviant". Society has many systems for those who are unable to fit in. Those who do not go by the rules may be ostracized, or may be placed in penal institutions or hospitalized for mental illness. For many others there is another kind of prison. This prison is replete with its own penalties and tortures: the prison of guilt. Those who suffer from unremitting guilt have become their own policemen, judge, jury and executioner. These individuals are far more severe with their sentencing than anything society would impose.

**NOTES**

# Meditation
# 1

Do you feel incompetent--defective--embarrassed about yourself; that somehow you are fundamentally flawed? If you do, you, along with many others, suffer from the problem of shame. This is a very large roadblock to recovery of self-esteem. If this problem is not resolved, it is impossible to live with any kind of validity or legitimacy as a person.

Shame is so powerful, it can paralyze. It can turn off emotion and prevent any authentic self-expression. It often leads to being chronically apologetic, perpetually meek and excessively approval seeking. It may manifest itself in an inability to carry out plans and act independently. Shame is usually reflected in harsh and unrelenting self-criticism. It is linked to our entire concept of what it is to be lovable as a person. Shame is so difficult to overcome because it is rooted in very early childhood experiences, a time when a basic sense of self is just beginning. This very early experience may be one of the factors responsible for self-destructive behavior as adults.

A case from my clinical experience comes to mind that illustrates the problem of shame. My client is a 38-year-old woman who complains of depression, marital problems and alcoholism. She was married to a successful developer, lived in an upscale neighborhood, had three beautiful children (the American Dream) and was totally miserable. In her words, "My life's a mess. I'm totally confused. I can't seem to enjoy anything. My husband doesn't love me, my kids resent me and my parents think I am just being stupid and need to grow up. No matter what I do. it ends up the same way, I'm miserable and I hate myself. I feel so damned stupid and incompetent."

Feeling incompetent. defective and embarrassed about herself, she had all the symptoms of shame. She was caught in a vicious circle of self-hatred leading to self-destructive behavior resulting in self-hatred, etc..

My client was raised in a large family headed by two alcoholic parents. She told me, "Mother never had time for me and Dad was always traveling." Though she did well in school, nothing she ever did felt like it was good enough. This pervasive feeling affects all of her efforts. Shame pervades her very soul.

The problem of shame undermined her self-esteem as well as relationships, If she feels fundamentally unlovable, how will she ever have a successful relationship? Because of a hunger for love, she tries desperately to please others. She is thus overly compliant and excessively nice and she bends over backwards to please others. This results in resentment because she doesn't feel appreciated and often feels that others have taken advantage of her.

In her family she did not learn to say no and was not praised for her growing independence and autonomy. If her emerging independence had been praised, supported and nurtured, she would have gained confidence. But instead, she was shamed, humiliated and embarrassed. There was an acute lowering of her self-esteem. She was very vulnerable at this stage. Her need for approval undermined her need for autonomy. Thus her conflict between the need for mastery and the need for love.

Shame at this critical juncture feels like an internal

hemorrhage. The child is made to feel small, helpless. needy, dependent and somehow defective in character. As if it is wrong to want to be powerful and independent.

In her case shame led to feeling defective. exposed, vulnerable and unable to love and be loved, she turned to medicating the pain just like everyone else in the family. What is the antidote?

The solution to this problem. like all solutions, begins with awareness and recognition of its seriousness. Because shame originates at such an early age. it can often be difficult to resolve. The goal is to create an entirely new self-attitude, To learn to love oneself, to enjoy being competent and to give up self-criticism are the goals. Confronting feelings and working through old wounds is never easy, although it is an essential step on the road to recovery. The journey of recovery always begins with learning to overcome shame by developing realistic expectations, more loving and compassionate self-talk, self-acceptance, and autonomy.

**NOTES**

# Meditation

# 2

Guilt is one of those very perplexing human experiences which has both a positive, growth enhancing and life affirming quality as well as a very destructive and life destroying aspect to it. It is something which is very necessary for society to function at all and yet it can totally inhibit and destroy an individual when it is distorted. Clearly, guilt and self-esteem are related because people who suffer from low self-esteem often have a great deal of guilt which makes it difficult for them to feel good about themselves. How might self-esteem and guilt be related in a positive, life enhancing way? Perhaps this will illustrate the function of guilt in both its positive and negative aspects.

He is a 50 year old man who is a minister by vocation. He, of all people, ought to know how guilt works and what to do with it. I have been seeing him for several months now and he came in and told me the most interesting thing. He had gone on vacation to Oregon to visit his family. One of the issues he struggles with is being able to like himself and feel free from a terrible feeling of guilt he has carried around since he was a teenager. The two factors to which he attributes his guilt occurred at about that time. The first incident occurred when he came home from school one day and discovered that his father had moved out. His mother, he felt, implied that it was because of him. Whatever the reality of that event, his psychological reality was that he had done something which caused his father to abandon him and the rest of the family. Several months later another event occurred which deepened his sense of guilt. He was pushing his younger sister in a swing and she lost her balance and fell out. She struck her head and was in a coma for several weeks. She recovered but has had some lasting neurological problems.

Twenty five years later he is still torturing himself about these events. His father has since died, taking with him whatever were the real reasons for his leaving the family. His sister, however, is still living and it was her that he went to see on his vacation. His goal was to talk with her, deal with his feelings of guilt, and ask for forgiveness. He did all of that. She sat and looked at him with compassion. "You've been carrying that around with you all of these years," she asked? "How terrible, I never blamed you, I was the one who lost my balance and didn't hold on tight enough to the swing." At that moment he felt an enormous sense of relief. He described it as the dam breaking. "I have felt like a stagnant pond, dead, and unattractive," he revealed. "Now, I feel like a running river, full of energy and life." I think this is a very good metaphor for the problem of guilt and its effect on how we feel about ourselves and the toll it takes on all of our relationships. He had never been able to feel close to his sister because of the guilt he felt. He just knew she hated him and blamed him for what happened. He also knew his mother blamed him for his father's leaving. So all of these years he walked around like a man condemned. Perhaps it was this feeling which caused him to choose the vocation he did. A vocation devoted to the pursuit of forgiveness from sin and guilt.

Guilt has many effects. It changes how we feel about ourselves, and it certainly has an effect on how we feel about others and how we behave around them. It distorts perceptions and leads to faulty attributions about how others feel about us. It leads to deadness of feelings, saps our energy and leads to self-punishing behaviors. Often we spend our entire lives trying to atone for some nameless feeling of dread and guilt.

One observation that can be made about guilt is that it is often totally out of proportion to whatever event may have caused it. This is the neurotic component of guilt. I often see people who feel guilty for just being alive, they are extremely self-critical, self punitive, and totally lacking in joy. They have difficulty in forgiving themselves and are often extremely perfectionistic in their expectations of self and others. This is the unhealthy component of guilt. Is there a healthy aspect to guilt? How do we go about dealing with neurotic guilt? And how can we tell the difference?

Guilt has both a feeling as well as a cognitive dimension. In other words, guilt is composed of ideas as well as feelings. These ideas are learned originally from others; parents, teachers, friends, and cultural institutions. Most often our sense of right and wrong is learned from our parents as they interact with us on a daily basis. We learn in a thousand different ways what they want us to do. How we treat ourselves when we misbehave is usually an internalization of how they treated us. Freud called this internalized parent our *Superego*. Our superego does not have to be necessarily accurate, fair, or compassionate. In fact, it usually isn't. Our first task as adults is to develop our own set of values. In other words come to grips with all of the rules and injunctions we have received all of our lives and sort them out. Then it is up to us to adopt our own rules. Conscience is necessary. It is imperative to know what is right and wrong. It is also imperative to know what to do when we have violated our own conscience. Yes, in fact we are our own judge, jury and executioner. The question is what kind of judge are we going to be, and what kind of jury is going to hear our pleas for mercy, compassion and understanding.

A neurotic sense of guilt is characterized by its unreasonableness, its unfairness, cruelty, and unrelenting demand for penance. We can never do enough to appease a cruel superego. This is the first step; recognize the difference between our conscience and our superego. I do not think we can really have a conscience until we allow it to develop from within. Superego comes from outside, conscience comes from within. It is necessary to learn to listen to that very quiet voice from within that tells us how to be ourselves. That's the function of conscience. It tells us when we are not being ourselves. In this sense, when guilt comes from within it is a very healthy function. It is telling us when we are not actualizing our very own spirit. When we violate our very own and very best sense of our own true self then guilt is a very appropriate feeling. In this case it is very important to pay attention to this voice.

When I am living authentically, I will be like a stream of living water. I will feel alive, I will have energy and I will nourish not only myself but also the lives of those around me. Have you ever noticed how dead every thing is around a stagnant pond. There is no life within or around it.

And so my client has learned a valuable lesson. He has deepened his relationship with himself as well as renewed his relationship with his sister. His neurotic sense of guilt which was literally killing him is gone. He has learned how important it is to listen to the calm, quiet voice within which told him he needed to do something about his guilt. He took appropriate, realistic action, and took the risk of feeling embarrassed or criticized. He was rewarded by being renewed himself. I often think of this as a powerful lesson for me as I try to be more realistic in judging, criticizing, and forgiving myself. Compassion, acceptance, and forgiveness are the marks of a healthy conscience. A healthy conscience leads to life.

**NOTES**

# Meditation
## 3

"You shall know the truth and the truth will set you free." I heard these words many times as a small boy in Sunday school. We preach honesty and stress the importance of telling the truth. In spite of the fact that we know "honesty is the best policy", how many of us are relentlessly honest? I had an opportunity to look at this issue recently because of a couple of encounters with clients which raised the issue to a new level of awareness for me. The first was a conversation with a young man who was telling me about a marital problem. He described it as watching the door slam shut or the iron curtain falling. This was what happened when he told his wife how he felt about something which had been bothering him for a long time. He "knew" what would happen if he told her how he felt. He had been hiding the truth from her for a long time but felt like he finally had to tell her how he really felt. He knew he wasn't being honest with her by acting as if he really felt the way she did. The issue between them was "religion". His wife is a very devout, fundamentalist, Christian, he doesn't feel the way she does but has been going along with it to please her. He felt that he needed to be "honest with her" because he realized that he was creating a situation in the relationship where everything was a charade.

In the second situation, I have a client who is a pathological liar. He wouldn't know the truth if it hit him in the face, and it usually does. He lies to himself, to others, and can't figure out why his life is such a mess. He has had three relapses in the past year and is going through a divorce. He stopped seeing me and then after relapsing he calls up desperately asking for help. We make an appointment and then he doesn't keep it.

In the third situation a woman is sitting at a table with several members of her family at a banquet and begins telling her daughter in front of everyone that she thinks the daughter is in an abusive relationship and should get out. The woman later tells me that she has been reading about abuse and has decided to go on a "truth campaign". She isn't going to be dishonest anymore, she is tired of playing games with people.

I tell these three stories to illustrate that there are many ways of being dishonest and there are many ways of telling the truth. We all probably have trouble in this area: being truthful involves several layers. The first has to do with what I call **being the truth.** The first case it has to do with our relationships with others in which we feel free to be ourselves. In order to do this we need to feel safe and have confidence in our own worthiness. Usually when we are not "being ourselves" we are being controlled by fear and shame, Fear of rejection, fear of retaliation, fear of exposure, these all come from the experience of learning that we will experience pain if we reveal our true feelings. As children we learned very quickly that by lying or pretending i.e., playing charades, that we could escape negative consequences and even get people to likes us just by being the way they wanted us to be. Usually this was done because we felt small and powerless and exposed. Charades serve to even the table. As children we are very pragmatic. We learn to do what works and seldom worry about long term consequences. Truth, justice, love and righteousness seem to be things that adults about. In essence lying may help us get what we want in the short term and also may help us avoid some painful consequences. So, there is a payoff, lying works and that's why we do it. Fear, expediency, safety and preserving self-esteem are the basis for much of the dishonesty occurring in our relationships.

In the case of the young man, he faced a difficult problem. He realized that the longer he let the charade go on the more dishonest the relationship was becoming. Yet he faced a choice, he could be honest with himself and take the risk of revealing his dilemma to his wife and possibly losing her or keep his feelings to himself and continue the charade. In so doing he risked losing himself and living a lie.

For me, this seems to be the most fundamental aspect of truth. Knowing the truth and being the truth require strength and courage. When we avoid knowing the truth we set up the conditions for chaos. We start the process of blinding ourselves so that we do not have to feel the feeling, face the problem, and perhaps do what is necessary to solve the problem. We also fundamentally keep ourselves from being truly ourselves.

So the first step in deception begins with not wanting to know: I believe the term is DENIAL. I saw an interesting example of this just yesterday. A well publicized baseball player was suspended for spousal abuse. His previous two wives also came forward to charge him with abuse. The television reporter asked him about his problem. His reply: "What problem? There is no problem."

In the example of my client the pathological liar, he has been living lies for so long he does it automatically. He neither knows the truth, cares about the consequences, nor is willing to be truthful with anyone. He does not want to know the truth, be the truth or tell the truth. Consequently he has cut himself off at the root. He is a dead man walking. The tragedy is that he keeps sabotaging himself.

In the third example of the woman who is on a truth crusade, she feels a compulsion to tell the truth. Yet her manner is hostile and destructive. She publicly embarrassed her daughter, involved the rest of us in the intimacy of family problems in a public place and violated the unspoken rule of playing charades in public. It is what we do when we are in public, we pretend that everything is wonderful. So, is it a question of knowing when and where to lie? No wonder children have such a hard time catching on to all the subtle nuances of charades.

Know the truth, be the truth, tell the truth, these are important principles which, when they guide us lead to more authentic relationships with ourselves, others and finally in the way we live our lives. Truth when tempered with love and compassion can become the healing foundation for recovery. It is also the only way we can truly be ourselves.

# Meditation

# 4

One of the rewarding things about writing is that occasionaly someone will respond to what I have written. Such was the case on my last article about guilt. He felt that guilt was too destructive and too heavy for people who were trying to regain self-esteem. Basically his position was that "we are all doing the best we can so why talk about guilt." I would like to respond to this by discussing what I feel are both the problems and constructive features that conscience plays in recovery. So, thank you Mac for taking the time and interest to share your reactions to my work.

First of all, what is guilt? Guilt is an inner sense of wrongdoing caused by our conscience. So, then, there are two issues, the first is the conscience and the second is what we decide to do about our guilt. The two are connected, because the kind of conscience we have will determine how we treat ourselves when we violate our sense of right and wrong.

I do not have time in this space to discuss all of the issues here, so let us focus on guilt. Guilt poses a major obstacle to recovery because it is so damaging to self-esteem. Guilt is both symptomatic of damaged self-esteem as well as a contributing cause to addiction in the first place. The position I take with regard to the role that self-esteem plays in substance abuse is that people with damaged self-esteem are at risk for addiction because they feel badly about themselves to begin with (a lot of shame and guilt) and often use substances as a way of coping with their lives. As the course of addiction progresses there is a circularity in self-esteem and substance abuse. A person feels badly about him/herself and uses to anesthetize the pain, experiences the consequences of abusing a substance, feels worse and increases the usage. This is how the downward spiral occurs. Guilt and shame both lead to addiction as well as pose a major obstacle to recovery. For this reason they must be dealt with in a very conscious and active manner. Not dealing with guilt and shame is part of denial. We don't want to feel the pain so we do not feel the feelings and avoid the whole problem of our behavior.

Perhaps we need new terminology to discuss this problem. I am trying to focus on guilt as a problem in recovery of self-esteem because I see guilt shifting to shame which becomes symptomatic of self-hatred and damaged self-esteem. Whatever we call it, we still need to find a way to restore our fundamental relationship with ourselves. This is where the transformation and healing needs to take place. I think we all agree that we need to learn to forgive ourselves and learn to accept ourselves as a basic condition of recovery. The question then is how we get to this place of being able to love ourselves in spite of feeling unlovable?

Step one, we are accountable. I do not agree that we are always doing the best we can and so should not be held responsible for our situation. I have behaved badly at times. I have not always made the best choices. I have done dumb and not very enlightened things which have had grave consequences for my life. I am still clearing up the wreckage of these decisions and choices. I feel embarrassed, stupid and guilty for hurting others by my activities. My life is diminished because I avoided responsibility and acted impulsively. There are lots of reasons for living my life the way I have. But regardless of my personal history, I am responsible for who and what I have become. I don't see this as an issue. The issue for me is what to do with the feelings of shame, remorse, guilt and diminished self-esteem when I face myself. As one of my clients said it, "how can I possibly love me after all that I have done?"

So, how does forgiveness, acceptance and reconciliation take place? I believe this has been a continual theme in all of my meditations on self-esteem since I have been writing for L.A. Steps. I believe the answer to this question is foundational to all recovery. I suggest that recovery begins when we break through denial and let the full weight of what we have been doing hit us. This is the first moment of enlightenment. We must realize and face up to the fact that what we have been doing is not working! The pain of this discovery can be overwhelming and painful. Sometimes it feels like it is too much to bear. Along with all of the consequences of substance abuse, we have the problem of hating ourselves to deal with as well. There may also be the problem of others hating us. The words loser, drunk, addict, failure, flake and bum in our culture all serve to label the substance abuser. We often internalize these labels and use them against ourselves as well. Here is where there is a need for a healthy conscience. One that is compassionate instead of condemning.

So, after the dawning revelation of our predicament hits us, what will be our response? This is where the first change must take place. What is needed is a new way of viewing ourselves. We must begin a new relationship with ourselves. What will this be like? The most meaningful word I can use is **Compassion**. As I struggle to regain my life and my self-esteem I endeavor to view myself differently. Instead of judging, criticizing, labeling, and rejecting myself for being me: using conscience as a club with which to beat myself. Conscience must be transformed within a new framework: the new framework is compassion. This means that I must now regard myself without judgment and condemnation. I try to love myself without conditions of worth attached. I let myself be! This is essential for **Acceptance**. Turning the tyrant of conscience into an enlightened guide is the foundationa of healing.

I was having coffee yesterday with a minister friend and he said to me, "tell me about forgiveness." I laughed. He wanted me to tell him about the most central teaching of his ministry. How ironic. He said most of his parishioners had a hard time forgiving themselves. I had to agree with him. It is a stumbling block with most people.

And so I talked with him about changing our way of seeing ourselves by changing our expectations. I talked about changing our internal self-talk from hostility and criticism to love and affirmation.and I talked about the need for inner healing which begins with reconciling ourselves to who we are. And finally I talked about the inner journey which begins with understanding ourselves and leads to greater awareness of our humanity and brokenness. That we must extend grace, love and compassion where there has been none before. When we can do this, the miracle of transformation is well under way. Guilt is only useful if we respond to it in a constructive way. It is only useful if it comes from the still small voice within which urges us on toward wholeness and warns us that we are always in danger of going off course. The more I appreciate the dangers, the more enlightened and whole I become. Conscience should not be a club, but rather a guide to healing. Guilt is the messenger that we are going off course. In this sense it can be the first step in recovery not an obstacle.

**NOTES**

# 8

# IDENTITY

Identity, that core sense of self, is the most central factor in determining the course of our lives. We live out our sense of identity in numerous and complex ways: in relationship to ourselves and others, career choices, and as we strive to fulfill our dreams. Living with a sense of satisfaction and fulfillment is the most challenging experience any of us will face. Every day, as our daily journey unfolds, our identity is at risk. When we are unable to live our lives in accordance with our basic identity we develop distress.

If the distress reaches very uncomfortable levels over time we may reach a crisis of identity. This is manifested in many different ways. Some of my clients have stated it this way, "I don't know who I am," others say, "I feel so lost and confused, I can't seem to find myself." When we feel threatened in our identity, we feel intense anxiety because our core self is at stake. When we feel unable to control our world, helpless to meet basic needs, or be the kind of person we have envisioned, despair or depression may result. Many of our difficulties in life are a result of how we try to manage these threats to our identity.

Crises of identity have reached epidemic proportions because of the kind of culture we live in. Large, industrialized, anonymous, cultures lend themselves to impersonality and lack of intimacy. They do not create the conditions which make for sound identity formation. So, instead of people being grounded in a solid sense of identity and community, they live with uncertainty and are continually looking for ways to feel significant, purposeful, and meaningfully connected to others.

Maintaining our sense of identity in a complex, accelerated culture has recently been chronicled in a movie called, "Grand Canyon." The characters are depicted as frightened, lost and harassed; all looking for that same thing, certainty and control over their lives. As they experience all of the catastrophes of daily life in the big city, earthquakes, violence, divorce, death, financial insecurity, and career disappointment, they struggle to love and get connected in some meaningful way.

To have a sense of identity means in part to be somebody to someone. We gain a large portion of our identity from our attachments and relationships. Because of the great deal of anxiety associated with finding ourselves, this has come to be known as the age of identity. It is a preoccupation which is not only chronicled in the movies, but it is also reflected in songs and other forms of popular culture.

Identity and various forms of crises have been a professional as well as a personal preoccupation for many years. My fascination has led me to investigate the complex roots of identity. To really understand identity, I have concluded, one has to look at sociology, anthropology, psychology and mythology. All of this is filtered through our present culture and finds its focus in the lives of unique individuals. Because we are so complex and preoccupied, most people do not think too much about the issue until a problem develops. It only becomes a problem when we can't seem to sustain our identity. Then, as our anxiety or despair mounts, we struggle to find solutions.

These problems are often manifested symptomatically in broken relationships, inability to find satisfaction in life, a sense of emptiness, boredom, or restlessness. Increased alcohol and drug consumption may be used to quiet the uneasy feeling that something is missing. This occurs when life stops making sense and the things which once were satisfying, no longer mean anything. In a crisis of identity, there is a growing sense of disappointment captured in the poignant phrase, "is this all there is?"

Identity, then, is that particular, very personal, window on the world which makes a person totally unique. Our identity is like a thumb print. Each of us views the world from a completely subjective vantage point. The vantage point of "I". This is what is meant by *Identity*.

I am often asked, "Why bother trying to understand all of this stuff?" I have so many people say to me, "Oh, that happened a long time ago, it doesn't bother me now, I have forgotten all about that." This too easily slights the importance of identity as an issue. It is a form of denial which would write off early experiences because they may in fact be too painful to face. My intent in this section is to help readers understand the evolution of identity as it works its way out through life stages, and perhaps the role it plays in the development of addiction. Perhaps, then, in this sense we can see addiction as a failed attempt to find and sustain identity.

# NOTES

# Meditation
# 1

My father died five years ago. He gave me his guitar, a Gibson made in 1915. It carries with it a lot of memories of him playing and singing with his brother at the Reece family reunions when I was a small boy. And now, I have his guitar, as well as my memories. I have been thinking about my father's legacy over the years. In my therapy I tried to come to grips with him. And I have also worked with several men who needed to deal with father issues. I should also add that it isn't just men who have father issues. "Dad," that word stirs so many feelings, images and memories in us all. My father was an alcoholic who got sober very early in my life, but he never got beyond that. My struggle with my father was fundamental to working out the identity question. In order to answer this question I had to begin with my father.

There are all kinds of father wounds. Over the years, I have seen brutal fathers, absent fathers, incestuous fathers, passive ineffectual fathers, controlling, demanding, domineering fathers and alcoholic fathers. In some cases fathers who were all of the above. I can't remember ever seeing a client who had a father problem who didn't have serious identity and self-esteem problems.

Robert Blye, in his warm and provocative book "Iron John", states that the greatest loss of the industrial revolution was the loss of fathers to their families. Dad goes off to work and when he comes home he only wants to be left alone. He gives his family his anger and unhappiness. And now that mom has gone off to work we may be seeing the same thing with mothers and families.

Fathers have a powerful effect on a child's self-esteem. The first and most obvious effect comes from the way the father treats the child. The child's basic sense of worth and self, in part, comes from this interaction. Mother's role is also significant in this regard and that will be the topic of a later article. But my focus here is the legacy of fathers to self-esteem. My father belittled, demeaned and criticized me. His primary way of relating was in shaming me. What did I learn about myself in these interactions? I learned that I was fundamentally flawed: there was something about me that was unacceptable.

This was confirmed in a conversation I had with him as an adult. One day fter I had gotten my Ph.D. degree, I took him out to my office to show what I had accomplished. We sat in my office and started to talk; perhaps our first meaningful conversation, I hoped. "You know Joe, (he called me Joe, my mother called me Gary, they never agreed on anything) I feel like we missed each other when you were growing up." (long pause) "Yeah, Dad you are right, we weren't close." And then the clincher, "You know, I don't know what it was, but there was always something about you ...." he faltered to a stop. I sat there mute, there it was hanging right there between us. He blamed me! If I had somehow been different or better then maybe I could have won his approval and his love. So all my life I have struggled to achieve in order to redeem myself in his eyes.

Fathers have a profound effect on self-esteem not only by the way they treat us, but also by the way they behave. We learn how to interact with others by their example (modeling). I learned all of his dysfunctional ways of dealing with women, feelings, money and children. My father's guitar has come to symbolize our very complex relationship. His heritage is my heritage. His father was abusive and so he handed it down, father to son.

And so the question seems to be for all of us; what do we do about our personal histories? Are we to be like a guitar, handed down from one generation to the next; victims who allow others to play their tune on our strings? Or is there some other way to take the guitar and play a different tune, our own tune. One that is different than the one we were taught.

Transcending my father's legacy of emotional abuse has taken me all of my adult life. His imprint was felt largely in my relationship with my wife and children. But it also affected the way I related to my peers and my professors. Why? Because the deepest effect was on my relationship with me. When the belief that you are fundamentally flawed is at the core of your very self it becomes the dominant life motif; a self-fulfilling prophecy. I am no good therefore ......

The first step in becoming aware of this large Oedipal struggle began with the crushing knowledge that one of my professors thought I had an authority problem. Imagine that! I couldn't seem to please him. I couldn't help it if he was "just like my father." Awareness is the springboard to knowledge. As I began exploring my relationship with my father, it led me to discover all the subtle as well as more obvious ways I was like him. How I hated being like him! The self-hatred, anger, sarcasm, cynicism, and unhappiness all mirrored him. I even used work to avoid my family like he did.

The legacy of shame was the next step in my journey of self-discovery. To get started, I wrote an autobiography which yielded a great deal of understanding in regard to the dynamics of shame and how it affected my ability to love myself and others. Changing this is a major project because it entails developing a whole new relationship with yourself. I had to stop treating myself the way my father treated me. The first step in transforming this relationship began with listening to my self-talk and changing it. Instead of anger and ridicule, I focused on acceptance, affirmation and compassion. Secondly, I had to get realistic about my expectations for my performance. I had to learn to feel my feelings, including my dependency and weaknesses. In short, give myself permission to be, without shame. In this process it is important to permit ourselves to feel vulnerable, small and childlike; the very things for which I was ridiculed. Learning to play and enjoy myself have come much later in my transformation. My journey has not taken place in a vacuum or in isolation. A very significant part of breaking this legacy was a series of very positive adult male relationships (mentors). These men came into my life at crucial, transitional times. This did a great deal to create corrective emotional experiences for me. Their validation and affirmation supplanted the shame.

Finally, I have continued to actively seek out male friendships so that I could learn to enjoy feeling like one of the boys and becoming a man amongst men. I am still my father's son. I still have his guitar, his genes, and his temperament. But I am also playing a different tune. My legacy is and will be significantly different from my father's. For this I have many to thank; friends, family, and mentors who cared in spite of myself. Love is a very old tune but whenever it is played it strikes a resonant chord and becomes a marvelous, magically redeeming melody. One with which others who touch our lives may also hearn to resonate and harmonize.

**NOTES**

# Meditation

# 2

    I was driving to Santa Barbara, listening to some Miles Davis and Mozart and my mind was free wheeling as it often does when I am driving. The occasion was my daughter's wedding. I found myself musing over all the steps that had led up to that particular moment in time. Two weeks earlier I had made the same trip to celebrate her graduation from college. We were passing a lot of milestones in a short amount of time. These kinds of events lead to my taking a few rolls of film to record it for our family history. The family photo album is full of moments frozen in time.

    I got to wondering about defining moments. I wondered if this was one. I also wondered what makes a defining moment distinguishable from all other moments. There are so many moments, in fact, most of the moments in our lives go unnoticed. These are not in the family album. Moments of dread, tedium, terror, rage, shame, boredom, despair and emptiness often go unmemorialized. Yet, these also form the unbroken chain of being we call our lives. Can we separate out one particular link in the chain and make it more important than the others? What gives our lives the special character that is as unique as our DNA Code? These questions floated by my mind's eye, like billboards on the coast highway.

    Another image came to mind. My mother had given both my children and me handmade quilts for Christmas a long time ago. As I looked at them I saw bits and pieces of clothing I had worn as a child. Like so many people born and raised in the first part of this century she never threw anything away. Clothing, string, plastic bags, aluminum foil and rubber bands; she was recycling things years before it was fashionable. She was a survivalist.

Her gift of love seems to be to be a better metaphor for what we call "defining moments" than does a photo album. Though she put together a crazy quilt of unmatched pieces of fabric she did it with care and skill and most importantly she gave it with love. Perhaps it was a love I found embarrassing or "quaint" because it was my mother's way and I had so many unresolved feelings about her. But it was her way. It defined her.

It seems to me that's the way life is. A crazy quilt of bits and pieces of experience which become the fabric of our lives. We are only able to detect a pattern if we are able to step back and reflect on the memories and images that emerge. We like to have the illusion of being the one who is designing the quilt and feel frustrated when we can't seem to make the design come out the way we want. If only we had the right materials or circumstances! Or when life hands us a whole bunch of colors we don't like, or tears a big hole, or when we almost destroy it out of indifference or neglect; we feel victims of fate.

John Lennon said "life is what happens to us while we're making other plans. We go along, often oblivious to the moments as they slip by like lines on the highway. Or we try to wipe out our consciousness because we don't want to be aware of the journey. This too, defines us. It seems whether we act or don't, plan or not, are aware or not, everything defines us. We end up stringing together a bunch of defining moments and that's who we are.

Occasionally we get out the photo album and look at ourselves frozen in time and we remember. Sometimes the memories are poignant, sometimes humorous and sometimes blurred when we can't remember a face or an event. Milestones, crossroads, peak experiences, defining moments: the pieces of a crazy quilt.

What seems to matter to me most is when I am able to put together some pieces with care and skill and give them away in acts of love. Perhaps my mother gave me more that she knew and certainly more than I was aware of until now. What a shocking and amazing thought!

Perhaps that I am able to see this subtle pattern in my life now is the signal that I am seeing my own history with greater clarity and perspective. I hope that my children will look at me and my life with some clarity and charity as they get free of the entanglements of childhood and adolescence. I recognize now, that part of my self-esteem as an adult is the joy I get out of participating in a healthy and meaningful way in the lives of my children.

I walked my daughter down the isle and watched with pride as she and her husband said their vows to each other; ones they had written for themselves. We, and a room full of friends and family had put together another patch in the quilt. We added some richness of color and stitched it all together with all the skill and care we could muster at the time. We brought all the love we could bring to that moment in time and in that place. We celebrated, danced and ate the wedding feast. They went on a honeymoon to Hawaii, I went home. We'll keep celebrating these acts of love together and feast on them from time to time.

# Meditation

# 3

I was sitting in a corner preparing some corn for a bar-b-q. A friend was sitting across from me at the table and was fixing some carrot sticks for munching. His wife came up to him and started telling him how to make them prettier. They spent the next five minutes arguing over the shape of the carrots. What's going on here?

A client was telling me that he was irritated with his wife for leaving the paper in the driveway all day and he had to pick it up and bring it in. What's going on here?

I would walk through the house every night when I got home and turn off the lights in all of the rooms not in use and then go into the kitchen and close all of the cupboard doors my wife had left open. What's going on here?

A couple that I work with tell me this strange story. Every time he goes out of town she engages in a furious flurry of redecorating the house. When he returns he is furious that she didn't consult with him.

What's going on here? These strange rituals seem to be a part of most relationships. Power, control, resentment, arguing and frustration are a volatile force in relationships and their effects are compounded over time. How are they related to self-esteem and identity?

I believe that the dominant motivation in the human personality is to self-actualize. To me this means that we are always striving to develop, sustain, and enhance our basic sense of competence, significance, and meaning: our self-esteem. As I have written many times before, these are the fundamental dimensions of self-esteem: competence, attachment, meaning, and a sense of significance or worth. Attachment and power are the twin roots of identity. In other words, who we are as persons comes from our attachments or relationships and our personal competence or ability to be self-reliant. Power and love--autonomy and attachment--individuality and relationships these are the many facets of self-esteem. When our self-esteem is threatened or when we feel threatened by a situation or encounter with another we become defensive. Relationships pose both an opportunity and a risk. We meet our basic needs through relationships. This places us in a position of need or dependence on someone else. This is where the dynamic begins to heat up. The core dynamic in all of these situations I described is people struggling to preserve "face".

What was going on between my client and his wife that they were arguing about who should pick up the newspaper? What was really at stake here? Obviously the newspaper is a small object and whether it is in the house or the driveway is rather irrelevant. But not to them! Somehow who brought in the newspaper had to do with saving face. It had to do with feeling loved and valued by the other and so it is manifested as a struggle over power and control.

Cupboard doors, carrots, and newspapers are the props on the stage where we act out the drama of self-esteem. It may take on the aspects of a high stakes drama, a sit-com, Trivial Pursuits, or Jeopardy. Each of us is playing a role which was scripted for us by someone off stage and a long time ago. We say the lines, we act out the play and experience the consequences; sometimes with deadly and or tragic consequences: most of the time without even being aware of the meaning of the play. In my case, the theme of the drama is "show me you love me".

Power struggles occur because of dependency, fear, lack of trust, need, and a sense of vulnerability. Anger gets tossed into the mix when we are frustrated in getting our needs met or somehow feel threatened or injured in the struggle. More often than not most people engage in these struggles automatically and without ever knowing why. They incorporate them into the daily rituals of their lives and do them unconsciously. "Who's Afraid of Virginia Woolf" is a classic example of two people held together by need and hostility. They are characterized as a gruesome twosome. We often wonder why two people would stay together if they are so miserable. They are bonded together out of fear and need. It is co-dependency taken to a ludicrous extreme. Yet there are elements of this in all of our relationships. How we accommodate ourselves to these situations reveals our personal style, our identity. Some retreat into isolation, others continually capitulate, and others engage in a running gun-battle. How we deal with power, control and love reveals a great deal about our personalities.

If we grew up in favorable circumstances in which people respected and loved each other and taught us how to do the same we were fortunate indeed. For others, learning to relate in more authentic-autonomous, less fearful and controlling ways, requires a great deal of work. In order to grow in these areas we have to learn to be in charge of our self-esteem, learn to love and accept ourselves, communicate our wants, needs, and feelings more directly, and accept the other as a separate person with equal rights. My client finally got around to telling his wife why he was bothered by the newspaper in the driveway. He was honest with her about his resentment, but more fundamentally he was able to talk to her about his need to feel important to her. This was a breakthrough for him because he had so much fear, shame and guilt associated with needing love. By reaching across the chasm of resentment and fear, he began to build a bridge to intimacy. Through awareness and honesty they were able to replace fear with trust: control was replaced by acceptance, and resentment was replaced with respect. Through communication they were able to be powerful and loving at the same time. What an adventure! Newspapers, carrot sticks and cupboard doors lose their significance when we learn to relate more authentically.

**NOTES**

# Meditation

# 4

    I drove down to Laguna Beach the other day to spend some time with a friend and unwind. I took a walk down to the tide pools and just enjoyed the experience of not having to do anything but be there and enjoy myself. I found a comfortable spot to sit and take in everything around me. This is my way of getting into a state of semi-meditation. I just sit quietly and let my mind and body slow down. So I was just sitting; birds flying, waves crashing, sailboats sailing, clouds passing, children building sand castles, and people playing in the waves. In my peaceful surveillance my eye was captured by a scene. A father and son playing in the surf with a boogie board. An ordinary scene on an ordinary summer day, yet there was something about this little drama which captivated my interest. I continued to watch.

    The boy was probably 5 or 6 years old. The father placed him on the board, held him firmly in place, and began pushing the board out into deeper water. A wave would come and he would take the board into it and then let it pass. Then he gently pushed the board under an oncoming wave. Supporting, protecting, exposing, teaching, guiding, encouraging, risking, and playing all in a seemingly natural and joyful way. That was what was holding my interest. A father playing with his son. A new wave came. He turned the board, timed his release and gave his son up to the adventure. His son held on, rode the wave all the way to the shore and then jumped up and raised his arms in triumph. His smile, joy and exuberance were a wonder to behold. His father yelled to him, "way to go, first wave!" There he stood, on the boundary of shore and ocean, boyhood and manhood. He had ridden his first wave and tasted the joy and exhilaration of power, meeting danger and the thrill of testing the limits of his smallness against the bigness of the ocean.

I was so moved and captivated by this experience that I wrote a poem and then shared it with a group of men. Several men had tears in their eyes. We talked about what we had experienced vicariously through this father and son. One man said it very well, "My father was never that way with me." This was the note, the hook, the fascination which pulled me into this drama: a father and son being together in a joyous and loving way. I have had time to reflect on this experience now for a few weeks and as I continue to return to it it deepens in its wisdom for me. That's why I am sharing this now. Its implications for self-esteem I think are profound. In fact, I would see this brief interaction as a paradigm for the way to build self-esteem. Let's look at just a couple of implications found in **the first wave.**

The first and most obvious observation is that the father was present. Parental presence is extremely important for building self-esteem in children. This father was not sitting on the beach watching, or reading a book. He was there, involved; he was active in his presence. A second major factor of importance in this interaction is the quality of connectedness. Albert Bandura a social psychologist says that the single most important factor in parental behavior being a "life model" to their children is that they are warm and involved. This is just a complicated way of talking about bonding. It is common sense, children want to be loved and feel good about themselves. They respond well if a parent is warm, caring, and nurturant. Somehow this builds self-esteem. They respond poorly, with diminshed self-esteem if a parent is hostile, critical, demeaning, demanding, cold, and authoritarian.

How did the father go about teaching his son? He was in the water. He was holding the board. He was exposing his son to risk, but in small doses. He was protective and strongly present. He guided the experience and chose the circumstances where risk was minimized and success was possible. He released his son to the elements under controlled circumstances. I am sure all of this came naturally, and the father wasn't thinking about being a good father. He was being who he was with his son. This is a critical factor that parents often have a hard time with. How much protection and how much freedom is optimal? There was a lot of trust involved in this experience. The son was dependent on the father because he was in over his head. The father entrusted his son to the wave and also trusted his son's ability to master the situation.

This is an extremely important, foundational experience for self-esteem. Trust leads to confidence and mastery through exposure to risk. Our self-esteem is always at risk as we surf the waves of our lives. Willingness to take risks often depends on how much success we have had in the past. Self-esteem builders are those first wave experiences which occur in a context of hope, meaning, safety, nurturance, and caring. This particular father on this particular day demonstrated for me a powerful lesson on how to be with a son. Playful, present, caring, joyful, and unselfconscious. The topping on the cake was when the father celebrated his son's triumph. We all need someone standing by and encouraging us when the water gets deep and our boogie board seems awfully small. The waves look very big when we are alone. What a wonderful, exuberant and exhilarating experience when we have that first wave experience and someone is there to celebrate our success.

Often as adults we are alone and there isn't anyone there to do for us what this father was doing for his son. Yet, I still think this little scene has much to offer as a point of wisdom. The first is that we must recognize the fragility of our own self-esteem and learn how to do for ourselves what this father was doing for his son. Since my father was absent and always working I did not have him present. And when he was with me he was angry, critical, and demeaning. He did not respect my smallness, dependency, and lack of skills. He certainly did not provide opportunities for me to learn mastery! It has taken a long time for me to learn how to be present to myself in a caring, compassionate, and affirming way. It does not do us any good to have someone standing on the shore telling us how stupid and incompetent we are while we drown.

The second factor is one of trust and competence. Recovery and rebuilding our lives begins with rebuilding self-esteem. Small steps, and taking risks builds competence which leads to trusting ourselves. This is difficult to do alone. This is where we need to create a recovery environment that will do for us what this father was doing for his son; support, validate, encourage, and go in the water with us. We finally, still have to do it by ourselves. Having someone in the water with us can make a day at the beach one where we transform fear into self-esteem.

## First Wave

Curling wave
Circling seagull
Ocean breeze
Sunshine sparkling on the water
Sailboats on the horizon
Crashing surf
The boundary of shore and sea
Father and son wading out to meet the waves
Boogie board at the ready

Man, boy and technology venturing into the elements
He turns the board with his son into the wave
Holds him with his strength
Gently pushes him under and brings him back to the
surface. Exposing, teaching, supporting, protecting

He watches--turns the board with his son into the
wave
Releases him to the ocean--gives him up
His small body entrusted to the adventure

The son catches the wave and rides the crest all
the way to the shore

He stands triumphant!
Arms thrust high
Giant smile on his innocent face

His first wave--exuberance, joy, triumph
Standing on the boundary of shore and ocean
Boyhood and manhood

His father standing, smiling, knowing the joy of
triumph because he had ridden his own waves and
survived.

But a larger joy because he was celebrating
his son's First Wave

Father and son standing in a long line of
ancient traditions--father and son going forth
to conquer

Rites of passage

# NOTES

# 9

# RECOVERY

Recovery has become a very popular concept in the past two decades. It seems that everyone is a recovering......Like most popular concepts and movements recovery has come to mean everything and nothing; the precision of its meaning and underlying truths has become blurred or obscured over time. Like most things which mean all things to all people it may have lost its usefulness. Is it a movement, a religion, a special form of therapy, strictly limited to the 12 Step Community, or is it a generic term which simply means someone is getting over something? Just what is this thing called **Recovery** ? Is it possible to use the term with any sort of precision? And to use another popular phrase, can the term recovery be **Rehabilitated?**

The first question which comes to my mind when thinking about how people get over things is, recovery from what? There is, in my mind, a determining relationship between the problem and the hypothetical solution. Fundamentally, recovery presupposes a problem. The antidote or healing solution is a function of our model. The most common example of models and interventions is alcoholism. In the last century it was viewed as a **moral-spiritual problem.** Hence the solution was, by definition, salvation or a change of character. Treatment-rehabilitation-interventions followed from these basic presuppositional biases.

With mental illness we see the same phenomenon; treatment follows from a paradigm, a model which has a whole series of assumptions about what "derangement" is all about. Is it a moral condition, as in sin or demon possession, social deviance, learned maladaptive behavior, a bio-psycho-social abnormality, or a disease? Answers to these questions lead naturally to interventions which are logically related to the propositions about what ails us.

Recovery, then, is a function of our paradigm or understanding of the problems under discussion. This understanding in order to be useful should reflect adequately the complexity (multi-determined) nature of the areas affected by the problem. This, in my view, rarely happens. Let us look at some examples of people undergoing ordinary life situations to see if perhaps *Recovery* as a generic concept contributes to our understanding of the problems involved and leads to meaningful interventions. In order for a model to be useful, it must generate understanding of the problem as well as functional interventions. Recovery from what?

In my career as a therapist over the past twenty years, I have worked with people in a variety of situations, including both hospital and outpatient settings. I have seen the wide range of psychological problems to which humans are susceptible. In addition to my work in the field of substance abuse, more recently, I have been specializing in disaster and trauma work. As a result, I have had the privilege of responding to numerous Critical Incidents: the Chino Hills Murder, a plane crash at Burbank Airport, the Palm Springs Girl Scout bus crash, and numerous incidents at local schools. I have also had the opportunity to work with several Vietnam war veterans. Added to these very public occurrences are the hundreds of victims of violent crimes and domestic abuse with whom I have worked. It is becoming increasingly clear to me that there is a similarity in profiles amongst all of these disparate people and situations. Shock, depression, flashbacks, confusion, psychological deadness, physical illnesses, sleep disorders, and disruption of daily lives characterize the cluster of symptoms known as "Post Traumatic Stress Reaction." The victims of disaster and trauma appear very similar in their suffering to clients with whom I have been working in the more traditional clinical setting of therapy; those who have been victimized by early childhood abuse. Their differences are mostly a matter of degree and the individual ways in which they have responded to their unique situations.

The impact of sudden, overwhelming, experiences, which render us helpless and shred the fabric of our lives, have a traumatizing effect that may last a lifetime. Trauma comes in many forms: plane crashes, earthquakes, flood, fire, war, terrorist activities, mass murder, civil unrest, nuclear accidents and chemical spills. People are traumatized daily by rape, robbery, drive-by shootings, bus crashes and economic hardship. It seems the list of traumatic experiences is potentially endless. If we live long enough, we might eventually experience many of these things. Though these experiences do not fall under the umbrella of Mental Disorders, they do in fact present terrible problems in living and have serious mental health consequences.

To live is to experience pain, loss and suffering. This is a common thread of our humanity. When trauma becomes personal, and we become a victim, it takes on a much different character; we experience the world from a perspective altered by our suffering. The world, once you have been victimized, no longer feels safe.

Our relationships with others take on another character altogether. When we have been traumatized intentionally by another, or in a seemingly random "Act of God", the world is never the same again. People are thrust into this new dimension in many ways, the common determinant is helplessness; being overwhelmed by circumstances which is characterized by loss of control. Trauma with the most long lasting psychological effects is when we are intentionally harmed by a person whom we have known and trusted. The majority of wounding then, in spite of natural and technological disasters is suffered by people within families and between people who know each other. Murder, rape, incest, child and spousal abuse comprise the greater part of trauma inflicted by people on each other. And as I continue to think about this issue of Recovery I have also come to see that people who suffer from the problem of addiction and substance abuse fit these parameters as well.

As I have worked with all of these varied populations and seemingly different kinds of problems I have come to the conclusion that this multitude, this conglomerate of vexing problems is just life. I have decided that suffering, loss, death, depression, anxiety and catastrophe are the ongoing stuff of existence. It is not what happens to us, because we are all subject to the human condition which is characterized by mystery, enigma, paradox, and tragedy, but rather our reactions to it and what we do about it. Even though every person with whom I work is unique in their particular history and manner of suffering, they have many things in common. They appear different in only the degree, complexity, and duration of their difficulties as well as their individual response to their circumstances.

Besides the commonality in suffering, I see a common thread in patterns of recovery. It seems then, we have two problems which are interdependent. The first is the enormous scope of traumatizing circumstances and secondly, the difficulty which people have in normalizing their lives because of (1) lack of information, (2) necessary follow-up, and (3) a recovery environment which promotes healing. It occurs to me that things could be improved considerably if there were a way to make recovery more systematic and available to more people. But, again, recovery from what?

It is clear that the unifying experience through all of these problems is helplessness in the face of life changing circumstances. We have all, at some time, felt helpless. When we reflect on those times, we can identify with almost anyone we have seen interviewed at a disaster site: their faces reveal outrage, shock, a sense of violation, numbness, terror, helplessness, and vulnerability. The world, for that moment, has been turned upside-down, they have become destiny's hostage. The moment of trauma leaves a person knowing that their world will never be the same. It is truly a "stop the world" experience.

Psychological trauma, in brief, leaves people deeply affected in several areas. Their basic assumptions about the meaningfulness, order, justice, and benevolence of the universe are often shattered. Their sense of significance and worth may be compromised, leaving them with an enhanced sense of shame and guilt. Trauma creates an intensely emotional experience which often leaves its victims numb, depressed, or chronically anxious.

The overloading of the psyche can also impact the body and produce psychosomatic effects that are difficult to treat with the usual medical interventions. Trauma also disrupts relationships and family networks in ways that cause concentric circles of victimization.

Attempts to normalize life after trauma may lead to secondary problems, depending on the appropriateness of care and knowledge the victims have about critical risk factors involved in the trauma. Trauma may exacerbate old wounds and overwhelm defenses. The manner in which we respond to trauma is a function of previous learning, current situation, and resources available to the person traumatized.

An example from my own experience illustrates this very point. I remember it with indelible clarity. It was a warm, sunny, Sunday California morning in 1972. I was teaching a class on family relationships at a local church when the phone call came. My wife was hysterical, she cried into the phone, "come home, Nickie is dead:" My wife had gone into the nursery to find our 6 month old daughter dead. She had been put to bed the night before apparently healthy. The cause, we found out later, was **Sudden Infant Death Syndrome."** (SIDS) I raced home to find the street teeming with police, fire and ambulances; the usual response to a 911 call. I remember clearly the coroner removing the body in a maroon satchel and being left alone with my wife and two other children, aged 2 and 5. My wife and I were both desolate: shocked, and numbed beyond words or feeling. Our world was never the same again. Events like this happen to many people everyday. They are life altering, perhaps even life shattering. And for these people, and others like myself, there is often no thought given to recovery. There are many like me who, unaware of their problems, have never healed. They have not moved from the twilight world of victimization to that of a survivor. A new world characterized by hope and the ability to care about life again.

What can we learn from this? I think that, first, trauma, is a helpful way of looking at problems and generating a recovery model which has a highly utilitarian value. Secondly, that it may help us understand the recovery process by looking at traumatizing circumstances. If the problem is trauma, what then is recovery?

Traumatic events present a rather uniform constellation of problems. It seems to me, then, that if we systematically address all of the various presenting problems we may be able to create a comprehensive, multifaceted, multi-disciplinary recovery program. Recovery, I conclude, in order for it to be fully effective must be (1) based on a comprehensive understanding of the problem, (2) focused on a skill development-empowerment model, and (3) based on a holistic paradigm which helps to unify and further the healing of the total human being i.e., mind, body, and spirit. Trauma refers to the wounding of your emotions, spirit, will to live, beliefs, self-esteem and your security. Recovery must take into account the effects of the problem, which are:

A. *Emotional*--shock, grief, fear, depression, numbness, despair, and terror; B. *Cognitive*--loss of belief, shattered illusions, loss of meaning, and distorted views of self and others; C. *Self-esteem*--devalued sense of self, shame, guilt, feeling violated and soiled (victimized); D. *Relational*--broken relationships, lost trust, withdrawal, alienation, blaming, acting out and abuse, E. *Bodily*--the numerous physiological consequences of trauma, sleep disorders, hyper-vigilance and hyperactivity, irritability, etc. And finally, F. the *life disturbing* and disrupting and distorting after effects of the problem.

Let us look at some of the complexities involved in traumatic incidents to see if it might provide some helpful insights into the nature of recovery. Because the effects of trauma are so all encompassing, I believe that treatment strategies which address all of the affected areas will be the most beneficial. Since the cognitive aspects of trauma are so powerful, treatment-recovery strategies must facilitate integration of the traumatic event into a person's world view. The issues of why, why me, and, if only have to be given a framework for understanding. In my case, I had to revise my idea of God and the nature of reality. This is no easy task because these are the fundamental assumptions of everyone's personal reality.

Additionally, since our self-esteem is usually injured, we have to devote time discovering how to regain or, in some cases, develop self-esteem if it was not there to begin with. Another important aspect of recovery is learning effective ways of dealing with potent emotional issues. Shame, guilt, rage, terror, and grief are but just a few of the reactions that threaten to overwhelm victims. Unless we find a way to deal with these emotions, there is a very real danger of them becoming serious psychological disorders.

And finally, the literature is clear, what determines successful outcomes in a wide variety of problems is the quality of the recovery environment. This has powerful implications for how we go about helping people recover from any kind of problem. As mentioned, previously, our relationships and the people we care about are the secondary victims. They, too, need help. If appropriate care is made available, the relationship network can be transformed into a powerful healing support system. This environment must be characterized by safety, support, competence, compassion, caring, empathy, and knowledge and constancy.

I have explored the concept of recovery to see if it has any meaning or value as way of conceptualizing problems and generating useful interventions. I have taken the position that the term Recovery may be useful when it is carefully aligned with a fundamental understanding of the problem under consideration. I have suggested that traumatology provides a comprehensive framework for understanding recovery because there is a universality to the process of wounding and healing. It is the intensity of the experience which marks the uniqueness of the trauma. By devoting ourselves to greater efforts at understanding the very nature of traumatic injury we will also by necessity make gains in our generation of intervention strategies which will benefit everyone who is "in need of recovery". The recovery program will, of necessity, be adapted to the unique wound under consideration. Each person will benefit from a program uniquely suited to the demands of their situation. Caring recovery professionals will provide critical information, knowledgeable resources, competent and relevant intervention strategies, and a quality recovery environment. As individuals we all may at one time be in need of recovery: both wounded and healer. Recovery is how we respond to life when it goes upside down. It requires courage, faith, hope, commitment, caring and a healing community. As we confront the new reality of our post-trauma world, we stand at a crossroad. This is our defining moment, our heroic confrontation with life, which becomes our new identity. *Recovery is the journey that continues on after the wound.*

# NOTES

# Meditation
# 1

I have been fascinated for a long time with addiction. But recently my focus has been on its relationship to other similar concepts like fixation, fetish, and idolatry. The thought occurs to me that perhaps these might be just different words for the same process. As I looked them up in various dictionaries, one word which they all had in common in their definitions was *Obsession.*

It should come as no surprise that the very nature of addiction is defined by obsession. Everyone who has struggled with a persistent and pervasive urge to act or has had that mind numbing experience of having a word, song or phrase stuck in their mind, or has had to go back and see if they turned off the burner on the stove three times, knows what it is to be obsessed. It is important to understand obsessions because they help us unravel the mystery of why people engage in repetitive activities which most of the time lead to negative consequences.

We only have to watch the daily news to see evidence of prominent people losing their whole careers and fortunes by being addicted to various substances. This seemingly makes no sense, if you believe that one of the most powerful sources of motivation in the human personality is pleasure. If we are motivated to seek pleasure and avoid pain, whence addiction? Examining the scope and kinds of things and activities that fall under the name of fetish can be like spending the day in the freak show at the circus. Throughout history there have been many different fetishes and idols. In fact, we could do a whole historical analysis and examine the many strange things and activities that cultures get stuck on. I'm sure it would reveal a great deal about each age to know what their passions centered around.

How does this happen? How do our passions fixate on a particular object or activity? Actually, the mechanism is rather simple. If we use the paradigm of trauma I think it is possible to see the dynamics of fixation rather clearly. It should be noted that it is very common for people who have been traumatized to develop various kinds of addiction. The reasons for which will be seen shortly. In my own particular case, after the death of my daughter I began to engage in several compulsive behaviors. The first compulsion was to work. The second compulsion was spending money. And the third was sexual. Let's look at how these get started and see what they have in common. The first thing we need to look at is the particular person and his/her circumstances. I had just undergone a tremendous life shattering trauma. My self-esteem, beliefs, and life situation had been dramatically impacted. In short I was in pain, felt helpless, victimized, out of control and frightened, angry, and confused. This was the internal storm caused by the after effects of my ordeal. This is the first observation: life stress is a critical factor in developing obsessions because of several elements. The first is the physical and psychological level of arousal in the nervous system. The second factor is related to this level of arousal, when we are feeling this way, it is intolerable and we need to do something to restore order and control. The third is primarily psychological, it has to do with the issues of self-esteem. When we are dealt a blow to our self-esteem or are not able to meet our self-esteem needs in our usual fashion we try until we connect with something which works. This is the underlying process of developing compulsions, addictions, fixations, and idolatry. In each case, I was hurting, I discovered quite accidentally that I felt better and so I resorted to that solution the next time around. When I worked long hours I felt successful, in control, competent, needed, and valued. I was also rewarded with a larger income. Other benefits also came from working long hours, it kept me from thinking about myself and so I was able to avoid my pain. My compulsive spending occurred when I discovered how great it felt to buy a new car every time I was depressed. Again, we see the same process. Emotional pain, problem solving behavior, reward, and repetition whenever the problem occurs again.

This, in summary, is the formula for disaster as well as success. Addiction, compulsions, fixations, and idolatry are failed solutions. They are tactics which were employed at a particular time and that worked. They had a utilitarian value; so we adopted them at that particular time in our lives. Some addictions are socially acceptable and some are less destructive than others. But like all compulsions they are fueled by fear, anger, need, guilt, pleasure and the drive to complete the cycle. We add fuel to the engine that digs us deeper into destruction when we fight the process. The problem most people have experienced is that in trying to change an addiction or compulsion we experience greater turmoil because it is difficult to change and the new "solution" doesn't give us the same immediate gratification. At the root of compulsion is wounded self-esteem and our attempts to restore our lives to some sort of self-esteem and our attempts to restore our lives to some sort of equilibrium. It is critical to recovery what we choose as a solution and give ourselves to in an effort to rebuild our lives. This will determine whether it is an addiction, compulsion, fixation, fetish, or idolatry. The object of our devotion must be worthy of us and it must serve the purpose of preserving and actualizing self-esteem.

**NOTES**

# Meditation
# 2

"I have been on a rampage." These were the words of my client that I wrote about a few months ago under the title, Young, Hip and Hooked. A lot has happened since that last writing. He has stopped his usage of cocaine. Though he is well into a divorce from a wife who refused to stop using heroin, he is now facing the most difficult aspects of recovery: containing the pain and handling his feelings and impulses in new, less destructive ways. In short, he is confronted with the necessity to find some new solutions.

His rampage is fueled by a volatile combination of feelings: grief, anger, fear, guilt, need, sex, and self-esteem. These warring emotions push him to do all of the things he used to do to "feel better" He has realized that these old ways have brought him to the verge of self-destruction. Dave is trying to rebuild his life. He is facing the typical problems of someone in the early stages of recovery. He is undergoing maximum stress: physical, psychological, social, economic and career stressors are threatening to overwhelm him. His life is in shambles, IRS is hounding him, he is filing for bankruptcy, his wife is litigating the divorce for maximum support, and his self-esteem is at an all time low. Is it any wonder that he is on a rampage. He feels tremendous anger and helplessness, occasionally interspersed with suicidal feelings when he feels hopeless and directs his anger at himself.

One solution after another fails him. He has gone through

phases of spending money and sexual conquests. At least "I feel alive when I am with a woman."

Dave is learning that recovery is a hard road. He is learning that rebuilding his life is going to take a long time. He is also learning that most of the work of recovery begins after getting clean and sober. He is learning that recovery is an inside job. It has begun for him with the realization that he had problems long before his addiction to chemicals began. This lesson, slow in coming, because he blamed everyone else at first for his difficulties, is beginning to sink in. Our focus has been on creating a program which will work for him. He realizes he needs a great deal of support to get him through the craziness of these moments. He also has come to realize that recovery is going to take the rest of his life because recovery is a lifestyle solution. In other words, the way he was leading his life was what created the problem and he will have to create a new lifestyle which will not have such toxic side effects. In short the beginning of wisdom is recognizing that, "I am the problem".

Step one in this journey has to do with handling the intense storm of feelings which threaten to overwhelm him and lead to serious loss of impulse control i.e,, doing really stupid things which worsen his problems. This for him is a major task: it usually is for everyone in recovery because in my experience people with addiction problems have difficulty in feeling, recognizing and expressing their feelings constructively. In our sessions we spend a lot of time talking about feelings and how to express them. He is becoming less fearful and more trusting of his feeling life. This is probably more of an issue for men because we have been taught to suppress our feelings. "Real men don't cry, don't need, and don't let anyone know they can't handle things." This is the craziness that most men grow up with and it can be a major obstacle to recovery.

Step two in Dave's recovery is in regaining control of his life by taking responsibility for his finances. Money was another addiction. Spend, spend, spend every time you hurt, are angry or depressed, or feel helpless. Making and spending money in our culture is socially acceptable. We are measured by our bank accounts. Dave is trying to find a different measure for his self-esteem. He is trying to live from the inside out. Discovering sources of self-esteem from within is a slow process because it doesn't have the thundering excitement of a cocaine rush and it doesn't make him feel instantaneously powerful like sex and cocain together. In fact, taking charge of our lives, making good decisions, and delaying gratification is very hard work. It has long term consequences for self-esteem but the short term pain is often difficult to manage.

As one can see, recovery is complex, it takes a long time, requires patience, and is a lot of hard work. Usually it takes place when we have reached the worst place we have ever been in our lives. It is a series of small miracles which makes recovery possible. The hardest part is believing in miracles and working to make them happen.

# Meditation
# 3

Recovery is dependent on a very comprehensive understanding of the problems, risks and vulnerabilities of the person who is trying to rebuild a life. In George's case he had multiple problems. He came from a family which had several alcoholics on both sides of his family tree. He, himself had started his career as an alcoholic at an early age. Presently he has had several hospitalizations and relapses. He also has had periods of sobriety and has been quite successful in the business realm during those periods. The source of turmoil in his life now is his marriage. There is much to be learned from George's difficulties. He married shortly after getting out of the hospital. His wife did not want to live with him for a variety of reasons. So, for three years they were married, but lived in separate houses, he felt deeply hurt, resentful and rejected. Are you beginning to get a clue that perhaps there are some problems here? I'll give you another clue, Whenever they spent any significant time together, there would be a massive fight, and then guess what. Yes, that's right, he would relapse and go on a three month binge of self-destruction which would eventually leave him near death and on the verge of suicide. Would it be prudent to ask, what's going on here? The first observation we can make is that something in the relationship is not working. George has a very serious problem in his ability to tolerate marriage. Children of alcoholics grow up with a number of serious problems, not the least of which is their high potential for being alcoholics themselves. The first problem most of them have is that they are seriously impaired in their ability to love. Though desperately needy of love and hungry for acceptance, they characteristically self-destruct in their relationships. Why? Because having a stable, loving, relationship requires interpersonal skills which were never learned in childhood. Again, at the core of the inability to love is wounded self-esteem and trust. Alcoholics who raise children damage them in several ways. They don't provide a stable, consistently caring environment. They do not express appreciation and affection to their children and reward them for growing competence and independence. Typically children raised in alcoholic homes are raised in chaos. Chaos is not good for children. Children raised in chaos grow up to be chaotic adults.

Another deficiency is in the ability to manage conflict, hurt and anger. Typically alcoholic parents are not good models for conflict resolution. Anger is often expressed inappropriately in rages, abusive tirades, drinking, passive aggression, silence and sulking or avoidance. None of these behaviors leads to conflict resolution and problem solving. Relationships cannot be successful if we do not know how to fight directly and fairly. Intimacy is not possible without trust and the ability to express anger directly in a non-destructive manner.

We cannot get our needs met if we do not feel like we have rights. And this illuminates another area of deficiency in children of alcoholics. They have grown up with no boundaries and sense of their worth as a person. How can we legitimately stand up for ourselves if we do not feel worthy of love, respect and fair treatment?

Recovery in this case will require George to learn how to deal with his anger, communicate his feelings, and say what he wants and needs. Before he can do this he must begin to repair his own wounded self-esteem and be in charge of it himself. He has been seeking his recovery and solutions to his problems in the person he married. Clearly it is not working. She is not the solution to his self-esteem nor his recovery.

He will not be able to live without her, nor with her if he does not come to grips with his difficulties in relationships. He has had a hard time accepting the problem as his because he has found it very easy to focus on her as the problem. She is controlling, she is unpleasable, she is cold, she is angry, she is manipulative, she is rejecting, and so goes the litany of his complaints. "I can't trust her and when I am with her I feel so upset and crazy that I have to go and drink." So far he hasn't gotten the idea that it is his problem. He is going to divorce her and find the right woman. We see history repeating itself here. How many times do we have to run into this stone wall before we begin to get the message? Part of the legacy of the alcoholic family is the reality that this is the way it has always been and history keeps repeating itself. This is reality for George until he does something to change it.

# Meditation

# 4

He came to see me when he was eighteen years old. Or rather I should say that he was brought to me by his parents. When I saw him he was pale, weak, and thirty pounds under weight. he was so depressed he could hardly walk or talk. He had been steadily deteriorating at home over the entire summer. He was terrified of thoughts about wanting to kill his mother. Finally his parents sought help. He needed to be hospitalized in order to give him the initial care he needed to handle his problems. He was there for two months. And now he is thirty one years old and we celebrated our thirteenth anniversary. I have seen him on and off over the past few years. Occasionally he gets into a crisis and gives me a call to sort things out. We were reviewing our history together and talked about all of the progress he had made and where he thought the members of the "class of 84" were these days. That's the name he gives to all of the people he was in the hospital with.

Whenever I write anything about recovery I always think of Tom. To me he is the most remarkable young man because of what he has endured, how he has managed to overcome tremendous obstacles and how he is running his life now. There are a number of things I have learned in my relationship with Tom I would like to share with you because I find it so inspiring. The first is that I as a professional cannot often tell who is going to recover and who is not. When I saw Tom he was so fragile and had such difficulty in functioning that I recommended that be be put on total disability. We were kidding about how his greatest achievement was in making it from his bedroom to the living room to watch the Three Stooges. He was only able to tolerate this for a brief amount of time. His family was very discouraged and often felt like he was going to be this way the rest of his life. He was on three different kinds of psychiatric medication and nothing seemed to relieve his anxiety and his depression. Some of his medication made him worse. Finally we decided to take him off of it.

The only constant through all of this was our relationship and his family trying to support him and bring him to see me. I also saw them and focused on support for them as well as him. I didn't do anything really remarkable with Tom. Occasionally we would go to a park and play basketball, sometimes for ice cream and sometimes we just walked. It's hard to know what it is that works. Carl Rogers once looked at therapeutic outcomes and found that it wasn't what the therapist did, it was the quality of the relationship that makes the difference.

And I believe that is the point of this essay, recovery cannot be predicted. Sometimes we get in the way of helping others and sometimes they refuse our help. But there are some individuals who seem to connect and benefit from the relationship. There is a lot of support for the idea that the single most important ingredient in recovery is "the quality of the recovery environment,i.e., the quality of connections with other recovering people.

What this says to me is that in order to have a good chance at rebuilding your life you need quality people in it who are willing to hang with you over the long haul. A second turning point in Tom's recovery was when he was complaining of loneliness and I gave him the name of some Alanon groups. He went to a few meetings and found some people he could relate to and identify with. He has continued to use that as a a base of support and has developed a number of significant relationships there. His father was an alcoholic and yes, he came from a "dysfunctional family."

Tom has his own business now and he just ended a relationship that was not good for him. He lives on his own and is focusing on continuing to discover what he wants to do in his life. He continues to learn about how to handle relationships and has developed enough strength to handle the various crises of ordinary life. His biggest achievement is that he was able to move out of the family home and become self-reliant.

What have I learned from Tom? I learned that recovery is possible if a person wants it badly enough, is given a favorable environment and a supportive relationship that is constant and consistently caring. I learned that I should never underestimate a person no matter how wounded he or she may appear to be. This is why I am fascinated by recovery and think of the process as the Hero's Journey. Thank you Tom.

# NOTES

# 10

# FEAR

Many of the things which have been written about depression may also be true of anxiety. In fact, anxiety and depression often coincide. Anxiety is a disorder which affects approximately 5% of the population. The most common quality associated with anxiety is that people often try to cope with it by resorting to the use of central nervous system depressants such as alcohol and tranquilizers. As we have discussed, this connection frequently begins the process of chemical dependence. A solution which becomes a problem. In fact, the biggest problem with anxiety is that it leads to so many avoidance behaviors.

Anxiety is characterized by feelings of acute discomfort, apprehension, fearfulness, tension, and numerous somatic sensations. These may include several of the following: hot and cold flashes, dizziness, faintness, weakness, sweating, numbness, tingling sensations, muscle paralysis, heart palpitations, chest pain, shortness of breath, feelings of unreality, choking, a large lump in the throat, and a feeling of dread or of imminent catastrophe.

The distinction that I make between fear and anxiety is that anxiety is fear without an apparent object. We are afraid and don't know why. Whereas depression causes a slowing or numbing of feeling, behavior, and thinking, anxiety usually is manifested by central nervous system hyperactivity. Most people prefer depression to anxiety because depression does not threaten a loss of control. Because in anxiety there is an over arousal of the central nervous system, chemicals which depress the activity have very reinforcing properties. They help a person feel more comfortable and at the same time perpetuate avoidance.

Again, like depression, anxiety affects all ages and no one is immune from feeling anxious or fearful at times. Generally, anxiety symptoms are categorized into three classes. The first class of symptoms are **phobias**. In this category, anxiety is limited to fear of specific objects with specific avoidance patterns a person utilizes to control the anxiety. Fear of animals, closed spaces and public embarrassment are common phobias. For most people, this is not a very serious or disabling disorder because the specific situations or objects are easily avoided. These phobias often have their origins in childhood experiences or are a result of conditioning.

A second order of anxiety is the *generalized variety*. This is anxiety without a specific focus or more of a vague or free floating quality. Because the sufferer in this case is not able to locate the cause so easily, it is generally more difficult to accommodate oneself to this problem.

Generalized anxiety has historically been treated as a problem emerging from within the person's unconscious. As such, it usually stems from repression of early childhood trauma, and conflict over discharge of intense feelings and impulses. It is often difficult to know what it is exactly that is making us anxious because the signal of anxiety may be the result of very complex experiences. For example, a few years ago I was at a dentist office having my teeth cleaned and during the procedure I became so anxious that I broke into a cold sweat, felt incredibly trapped and immediately nauseous. It was so intolerable, I had to leave.

What was the meaning of this experience? This is the foremost question which comes to mind. If anxiety is an alarm signal, where was the danger? I was in a dentist's chair being cared for by a gentle, caring and competent dentist whom I had known for years. As I sought to understand the meaning of the "seemingly irrational," fear I made some important discoveries. The first was that lying on my back in a chair while I experienced the pain of someone working in my mouth I felt vulnerable, helpless and dependent. These are three very powerful triggers for anxiety, particularly if our psychological history has been problematic in these areas. And mine was! I had an abusive father who inflicted pain when I was dependent on him and helpless to do anything about it.

These very old, unconscious feelings were triggered by an immediate environmental stimulus. This is often the way it works, anxiety can be a blend of old and present experiences. That is why it is very important to pay attention to the experience no matter how seemingly irrational or "without any real reason" they might appear to be. Careful tracking of the experience can lead to important discoveries which will then make it possible to implement appropriate coping strategies.

A third form of anxiety is one which has been receiving a lot of attention lately. **Panic attacks** are a severe form of anxiety characterized by sudden onset, severity of symptoms and debilitating patterns of avoidance. Most people who have had a panic attack report almost uniformly that "it came out of the blue." Some even report that they were sleeping soundly and awoke terrified. This sudden onset is particularly disturbing because the symptoms occur in situations which have not previously caused any anxiety. People mistakenly, out of a need to explain the cause, attribute or associate the situation with the anxiety. They may be standing in line at the grocery store or the bank, or driving on the freeway when, suddenly, the anxiety begins. It then becomes associated with what they were doing. The symptoms are often so severe, because of the catastrophic expectations associated, that when they occur the person frequently seeks medical attention. Many who experience it think they are having a heart attack, may be going to die, lose control, go crazy or something else equally world ending.

Indeed, the mysterious onset, severity of the symptoms, and the associated physical sensations seem to be potentially lethal. The key here is *seem* to be. Since we all need to know what is going on and need to feel in control, this betrayal of the body is particularly terrifying. When a person discovers that by avoiding the freeway, bank, store, elevator, etc..., that the anxiety does not occur, it is a very natural tendency to seek control through avoidance. This secondary reaction of avoidance becomes a problem when anything which triggers anxiety serves as a new stimulus to anxiety. Hence, we now have a new phobia; fear of fear.

Anxiety, unlike depression, is easily generalized. This is a serious complication when one thing or another causes anxiety because the person begins avoiding more and more things. It may become so severe that the sufferer may be unable to get out of the house. For some, even the thought of becoming anxious triggers an attack. So a person becomes hyper-sensitized to any internal or external cue which has become associated with anxiety.

A variation of panic attacks which may occur with or without them is **Agoraphobia**. Agoraphobia is a fear of being in places or situations from which escape might be difficult or embarrassing. Closely related is a fear of not being able to get help, of being isolated, or alone. Common agoraphobic situations include being alone, traveling in a bus, plane, or car too far from home, being in crowds, or standing in lines. As mentioned previously, this problem has serious complications because as the person responds defensively, he/she often resorts to either avoidance or to using chemicals to cope with anxiety.

The causes of anxiety, phobias, and panic attacks, like depression are varied. Again, the debate rages between those who advocate the physical causes and those who lean toward psycho-social causes. The overall profile of the anxiety prone person has several common features. The first commonality is usually an anxious childhood where one or both parents were fearful or there were situational variables which promoted insecurity; like divorce, family instability, alcoholism, or abuse. This kind of history lends credibility to theories that there is a biological predisposition to anxiety proneness. The chicken or egg theory is problematic because if one is raised by anxious, unstable or alcoholic parents there is a strong likelihood of this creating problems for any child.

A second common feature is a recent history of severe or prolonged stress. This appears to have an effect on the nervous system which causes a lowering of the anxiety threshold or sensitizes the nervous system by overloading it. Finally, there may be a loss of attachment or self-esteem which threatens a person's security. When these three factors are found together, there is a high probability of an anxiety attack. I have found that the kind of anxiety and the course it takes is a function of each individuals unique history and biological heritage.

Like depression, anxiety has special meaning for the individual. Regardless of whether there is a physical predisposition, anxiety has the function of signaling danger. Anxiety is experienced when something is perceived either internally or externally that triggers the body's alarm system. Once the emergency response system is activated, a very predictable physiological response occurs. The person is now activated to either fight or flee. The problem becomes acute when the danger signal is not known and appropriate coping responses cannot be found or are not known. The result is the very uncomfortable sensation of being in acute danger and not knowing what to do to escape the danger; in other words, feeling helpless and out of control fuels the anxiety.

Coping with anxiety requires learning as much as possible. Because of the complexity, and various ways in which it affects each person differently, anxiety presents a challenge to both those who experience it and those who treat it. It has been found that a broad based approach which attacks anxiety on several fronts has the best chance of success. Just as in the case of depression, the starting place begins with **awareness.** It is particularly true in the case of anxiety that the more one can know about it the better one is able to cope. Knowing gives power and control over what was previously mysterious. Through *assessment* of the occurrence, the symptoms, the defenses and conditions which precede anxiety attacks certain patterns begin to emerge. Once these patterns become evident a course of action may be planned.

The first and most important thing to know about anxiety is that it is not lethal, nor does one go crazy from it. Even though it feels catastrophic, none of the things that are feared happen. Truly, the only thing to fear is anxiety itself. Therefore, education, frequent exposure, and reassurance are very important. A major factor in anxiety which tends to determine its course is *self-talk*. Once again, what determines our response is how we perceive the stimulus. Therefore, an important step in coping with anxiety is changing our thoughts about it. The first thought to change is its catastrophic nature. Do a reality check on the fears. What is the likelihood or probability of any of the feared consequences happening?

Checking the reality basis of fears leads to an important step. Listening to negative self-talk, this is a procedure to which we have referred several times. It is again applicable here. In this regard it is important to see how these feelings may be increased by negative self-talk. The most important thing is to develop awareness of the things which are told to oneself about the anxiety and one's ability to cope. Usually, the thoughts are undermining and devaluing of coping abilities. These thoughts need to be changed to realistic statements about the situation, the ability to cope and the probable outcome. These positive affirmations shut off the feelings of panic and helplessness which come from the perceived overwhelming nature of the catastrophe.

Besides awareness and cognitive modification, a third important coping technique is relaxation. Relaxation shuts off the emergency alarm system. One cannot be physically relaxed and anxious at the same time. It is impossible! Visualizing the feared situation while relaxed is a common form of systematic desensitization. It will help one to shut off the negative expectations and reduce the fear by de-conditioning it. Gradual self-exposure to feared objects and situations while relaxed is also another way to desensitize anxiety.

Finally, self-exploration in terms of one's early childhood experiences often leads to uncovering areas of vulnerability and the origination of many phobias and sources of anxiety. One measure of the strength of the self is the capacity to bear anxiety and depression. By increasing the overall ability to cope one gains self-confidence and self-esteem. This needs to be strongly rooted in knowledge of oneself.

In summary, anxiety may be dealt with by employing several strategies which encompass the cognitive, behavioral, and the emotional. Changing thoughts, negative self-talk, relaxation training, systematic desensitization, and self-understanding are all important to effectively cope with anxiety. Confronting avoidance by substituting more active and assertive behavior will increase self-esteem and decrease anxiety. Sometimes a course of anti-depressant medication along with behavioral interventions adds significantly to the successful treatment. Generally medications which suppress the central nervous system, i.e., tranquilizers and alcohol tend to create dependence and or addiction and for that reason are not viewed as good choices in terms of long term solutions.

# NOTES

# Meditation

# 1

Sam's anxiety had become so disabling that he was confined to a 5 mile radius around his house. Sam is a 55 year old man who has struggled with anxiety all of his life. His life is literally controlled by fear. Every decision he makes is in response to fear. His waking life is devoted to avoiding fear. He has gotten it under control by rigidly adhering to very precise rituals and daily schedules. When he deviates from this pattern he has a panic attack. He literally is a "child of fear."

Sam's mother was very fearful. She taught him at a very early age that life is a fearful place. Her daily admonitions told him to be careful, "watch out, don't do that you might get hurt, be careful, here, let me do that, you might hurt yourself, etc." She would never let him out of her sight. Overprotective is an understatement when it comes to her parenting style. His father was cold and ineffectual. He did not model strength, nor teach Sam how to cope with the daily problems of living. The family life was dominated and controlled by fear. Instead of learning how to cope with life, Sam's entire defensive structure was fear-based.

This is how Sam grew up, he learned how to control his fear by rigidly adhering to rituals and daily schedules which were predictable and controllable. He functioned adequately as long as there were no surprises. He actually had a somewhat normal life. He got a job with the phone company and was a very good technician. He liked working with objects which were controllable and that he could fix. He liked to tinker. This was a great diversion for him. He would spend his weekends taking apart old cars and motorcycles and restoring them.

Life was good for Sam until his wife grew tired of the rigidity and sameness and began drinking to alleviate her boredom. She developed a serious drinking problem and eventually died of alcoholism. This was a problem for Sam which he could not control by tinkering or ritualizing. His panic attacks erupted to the point that he could not get out of the house or get to work. One of the problems in treating some one with this kind of problem is in getting them to come to the office for sessions. I referred him for psychiatric evaluation and an anti-depressant was prescribed. This controlled the anxiety to the extent that he could get to the office and get back to work, The next task was to try to restore Sam to his previous levels of functioning. Notice that I did not talk about cure.

Sam is a classic case of how anxiety develops and its effects on a person's life. In him we can see the major features of anxiety. He was born and raised in a fear inducing environment. His biological heritage was probably genetically predisposed to be anxiety sensitive. And he also had major life stressors which overloaded his defenses. Here we see all of the factors: genetics, social learning, and life stressors.

The course of treatment for conditions which are fear-based is complicated. It requires a careful assessment of all the factors involved in its development and course in a person's life. Sam learned a great deal about his anxiety. He came to recognize the triggers, he discovered ways to control the symptoms by using his talents at tinkering and working on old cars. We focused on his self-talk and helped him to dispute the catastrophic thinking and realistically appraise the actual dangers of the moment. He became adept at employing various relaxation techniques when he felt the beginning warning signals of anxiety. All of these things are a part of learning to deal with anxiety. They are based on the simple idea that fear is a signal of danger. Sometimes it is a false alarm. The antidote for fear is empowerment. Anything you can do to put yourself in charge, take control and go through the anxiety will reduce the problem. The greatest danger of anxiety is to avoid it. Anxiety and fear get stronger and you get weaker when you do not actively face it Anxiety when not faced becomes a tyrant which can reduce the circle of your life down to one room if you let it. In the words of the movie "The Ghost and The Darkness, "Don't let fear build a home in your soul." That is the real key to living with fear. Know your adversary, confront it, and go through it not away from it. As you do this you will get stronger and it will get weaker. Be aware of your fearful thoughts and challenge them. We truly have nothing to fear but fear.

# Meditation

## 2

The experience of fear can be so powerful that people will do almost anything to escape the feeling. People have been known to commit suicide because their lives had become totally controlled by unrelenting fear. Anything which can alleviate this kind of suffering can have the same kind of power as the anxiety. That is why anxiety plays a key role in the development of many different addictions.

A young man came to see me because he had developed a dual addiction; pain killers and alcohol. He didn't even think of the alcohol as a problem because he didn't drink until he ran out of pain killers. When I first saw him, his speech was slurred, his thinking was very slowed, and his ideas were very disconnected. His primary complaint was that his wife was leaving him. "I am terrified of being alone Doc." I asked him what happened when he found out his wife was leaving him. He stated that he immediately thought, "Oh my God what am I going to do without her," and then he began to experience waves of anxiety. His fear was so great that he literally believed that he could not exist without her. He had been given some pain medication for a back problem he had gotten from a job injury and so he took some of that. He made a discovery, he felt less anxious. He took some more and felt even better. He soon discovered that the problem was kind of receding into the background of the haze he felt most of the time. The problem was that the doctors became rather stingy with their prescriptions and he couldn't always get as many pills as he wanted. So he filled in the gaps in his self-medicating regime with alcohol. This went on for a year. He not only lost his wife but also his job. He was on the verge of losing his health as well.

This is a familiar story. Psychological pain leading to physical pain which leads to chemical solutions which lead to even greater pain. Anxiety played a key role Jerry's story. His history was so familiar. His father was an alcoholic, his parents divorced when he was a teenager and he married early to escape the family problems. These are key factors in understanding Jerry's problem. They point to several risk factors which, when compounded reveal the profile of a vulnerable person. Family history of addiction, disruption and loss of family stability at a critical developmental period, major life stressors and utilization of chemicals to cope with the problems.

The anxiety he felt at his wife's announcement triggered feelings of separation and abandonment which evoked the pain of his earlier loss caused by his parents divorce. Jerry did not have inner resources to help him sustain the loss of his wife. He felt empty, lost and abandoned, like a small boy who had lost his mother. He had few psychological or social resources to sustain him during this crisis.

Jerry's anxiety and his dual addiction are not his problem, yes, they are a problem but they are symptomatic of his fundamental problem: his psychological impoverishment. His anxiety is telling him that he has not become an independently functioning adult male. He feels and acts like a small boy who needs someone to take care of him. He has not developed friendships, his self-esteem is totally dependent on his wife's affection, he has not developed a sense of competence and mastery in his life which puts him in charge of his self-esteem. Anxiety triggers feelings of worthlessness. "She does not love me, therefore I must not be lovable."

Recovery for Jerry will involve several steps. As we can plainly see, the first and most obvious step is giving up his chemical crutches. The problem here, of course, is that this will unleash the hounds. His anxiety will worsen because he won't be medicating it. He will need a great deal of support, and have a lot of work to do in the area of growing up. His anxiety is a message that he needs to solve the several problems he is confronted with. It is a wakeup call. Since I only saw him once for a consultation, I am not sure he was listening to his alarm clock. It will continue to ring, we can be sure of that. How much does he have to lose before he gets the idea that there is a problem and the problem is him? When he walked out of my office, his mother embraced him and helped him walk out to the car. I had the feeling that she was not about to let her little boy grow up. Perhaps, he was all she had. As Robert Blye so strikingly observes, "If little boys are to become men, they must steal the key to the cage that imprisons their manhood from underneath their mother's pillow."

# Meditation

## 3

How do you know you are doing the right thing? This question was asked by one woman in my group to another who was struggling with the decision to leave her husband. The woman wrestling with the decision has been stuck for quite a while now. A year ago she asked him to leave and so they sold their house and she got an apartment. Six months later he moved in with her and they worked on their relationship. Things were satisfactory for a while and now they are right back where they were when she asked him to leave the first time. Other questions were put to her about her situation, but the one which troubles her the most is, "How do I know that what I am doing is best for me?."

There are a lot of implications in this question. But underneath them all is the issue of her self-image and self-esteem. Sarah ran her litany of complaints by the group. They were basically all related to the same theme. "I do not feel cared for." The clincher, the test case, was that he had agreed to mop and wax the kitchen floor as part of his responsibility for household chores. He hasn't done it and she is furious. "Show me you love me" is a variant on "show me the money." Amongst the mundane, the trivial and the ordinary things of daily life our self-esteem is at risk. When we feel devalued, threatened, or unable to satisfactorily achieve our needs for affection and worth we experience very primitive emotions. Fear is one of the signals which lets us know we are in danger. Fear also has another function, a positive one. **Anxiety is a messenger that our basic self is at risk.** So, to answer the original question about how we know we are doing the right thing for us, I would say that we must pay attention to the signals which come from within. Now as we have seen in other examples fear is not always an accurate or reliable signal of our wellbeing. It can be exaggerated, false, or a barrier to freedom. Yet, with all of these disclaimers, anxiety does serve an important function.

In Sarah's case anxiety is acting as a barrier. She is staying in a relationship that intellectually she knows is toxic to her. She is afraid of not having a relationship. Her fear of being alone is keeping her stuck. We talked about this at great length. Someone observed to her that she had been here before the last time she left. "What's different this time?," someone asked. When you are with him you're miserable, and when you are on your own you aren't happy. This brought into recognition that she was the problem and that she was afraid to live her life the way she wanted because she didn't trust herself. Fear of making a mistake, fear of being alone, fear of what others would think, fear of not having anyone there for her and fear of being old and alone. This aggregate of fear can be pretty daunting.

Sarah recognizes her dilemma in so far as she is committed to getting herself emotionally ready to do what she needs to do. In many ways this is like training for a triathelon. She needs to develop some psychological muscle to counteract the fear.

How does one do that? The first step is in letting the fear be her teacher. By listening to her fear she will learn about herself, she will learn what it is she is afraid of. Once she recognizes this she will then know what it is she needs to do to grow. It is, again to use the training model, like starting training and finding out how weak and out of shape you are. A rigorous assessment will soon let her know what she has to do to be ready to succeed in her new venture. If she is afraid of being alone, she must practice being alone. If she does not now how to meet her needs, she must discover what her needs are and systematically develop a way of doing it. Each area of weakness-fear, must be addressed and practiced in order to build skills which will help her meet her final goal.

Going through the fear is part of the exercise which will strengthen her. As she does this, her confidence will grow, she will learn to trust herself, and she will feel more competent and self-reliant. Her sense of what is right for her will come as she develops her inner compass. Most of us have not learned the skill of navigation through being inner directed. The cues and demands, the shoulds and expectations from others all cloud her personal horizon. Who is best to know what she wants and needs for her life? **It takes courage to pursue that lonely course of self-determination which leads through the valley of fear, self-doubt, confusion and despair. The reward is self-discovery, self-esteem, and freedom.**

# Meditation

# 4

Fear operates at many levels and in many different ways, that is why it is so difficult to manage. The key to managing fear is to understand both its *origin* as well as its *function*. Let's look at the case of Joan to illustrate what I mean. Joan is a woman in her 40's who is highly educated and is a minister by profession  She is married and her husband is also a minister. Three years ago Joan was working late at her church office in an urban area. A man broke in and assaulted Joan, he carved a swastika on her stomach. Joan has not been able to work since that time. Her condition is described as  Post Traumatic Stress Disorder, PTSD. PTSD is a condition caused by an "overwhelming experience of fear or terror caused by the exposure to harm, threat of death, or horror to either oneself or one's loved ones. The key phrases in trauma are exposure, being overwhelmed, and the threat of death,  harm, and horror. These kinds of experiences render us helpless in the face of harm. This is the recipe for fear, anxiety and terror. I usually think of these three terms as expressing gradations of fear; fear being the mildest and terror being the most extreme. It is clear what the origin of Joan's condition is. Assault on our person leaves us feeling vulnerable, violated, shocked, confused, angry, helpless, and very fearful. This condition is known as "victimization". When we are victimized the effects are profound and often life-changing. This is even more true if it is at the hands of another. Victimization often results in devalued self-esteem, shattered beliefs, damaged relationships, wounded spirit, and powerfully affected feelings. Our bodies often manifest the prolonged effects of overwhelming terror. Sleeplessness, irritability, fearfulness, disturbed appetite, being easily startled, headaches, upset stomach, fatigue, and hyper-vigilance (an experience of being extremely alert for danger). This is is the result of a powerful shock to our central nervous system. In computer terms, it has the effect of a "power surge.

Joan has not been able to work again because of this incident. The fear has affected her in several ways. There is a fear of **recurrence,** in other words people who have been victimized are afraid of it happening again. Most people walk around with a feeling of confidence and invulnerability. Incidents like this shatter that feeling. If it happened once, it could happen again. Overwhelming fear also affects us by lowering our threshold of tolerance. A third effect is that of the phenomenon of generalization. In other words, anything that vaguely is like or associated with the event has the power to trigger the same feelings all over again. Finally, fear undermines our sense of competence and mastery. Again, most of us walk about fairly confident in our ability to control our worlds and accomplish the tasks of daily living without the presence of fear or doubt. Victimization shatters this confidence and leaves the victim fearful of everything.

Recovery from PTSD is no easy matter, but I have found in my own experience as well as working with others that traumatic injury provides a helpful framework (paradigm) for understanding recovery in a larger domain. That is because in many ways people who have been damaged regardless of the cause often go through many of the same steps in rebuilding their lives. That is why I have chosen Joan's case to illustrate the process of recovery from fear based problems. Recovery for Joan has been a long and slow process. This is the first rule. The amount of damage determines length of recovery time. The second rule is that successful recovery is dependent on the quality of the recovery environment.

Judith Herman-Lewis a psychiatrist specializing in recovery states that the key to overcoming trauma is **empowerment**. By this she means that victimization is the problem. Therefore the solution is for the victim to regain the power, competence, and confidence which was taken away. This is the antidote for fear. We have to be in charge of our safety. We have to regain control of our lives. And we have to be in charge of anything which affects our self-esteem. Like Humpty Dumpty, the shattered self needs a lot of repair. We must be in charge of it, however, we may need all of the king's horses and men to help us recover. A supportive recovery environment where we feel safe, validated, understood and cared for is essential for combating the pervasive and powerful effects of fear The rest is just strategy (program) and practice. We rebuild one day at a time.

# NOTES

# 11

## LOVE

I was sitting under a Joshua tree in the Mojave Desert with a friend several years ago. It was one of my favorite activities. We would load up our motorcycles and our two teen age sons and head out for a day. Our sons would ride their bikes on the desert trails and my friend and I would sit and talk. Our conversations ranged across the broad topics of theology, philosophy and life in general. I began the conversation, "Don what do you think is responsible for the great evils in the world?" He pondered for a moment and then answered me by saying simply an eloquently, *"failure to love."* I sat there in silence. I thought we were going to have a conversation that would last for hours. In his own fashion he said all there needs to be said. And now as I sit and write this I reflect on our conversation and the tremendous irony of that day. One year ago after I had attended my daughter's wedding in Santa Barbara, I got a phone call from Don telling me that his son Randy's funeral was going to be the next day. Randy was murdered at work by the husband of a woman who just walked in; shot her, then Randy and then himself. Failure to love indeed! The sadness and irony are very painful for me. Don is my favorite person, a gentle, brilliant, sensitive, philosophical, cultured man. He has been my friend, mentor, and guru for 30 years. He and I have devoted our adult careers to helping people overcome the effects of brutality, abuse, and perversion to lead healthy lives. And his son was gunned down in a senseless, savage act of madness.

I would like to continue that conversation with Don in this chapter, a conversation which has been interrupted by 17 years and a number of tragedies. My reflections continue along the lines suggested by Don. Love gone wrong, love perverted and the relationship between love and power. Love and power, are in my view, tremendously important dimensions of self-esteem.

First of all, I concur with Don that much of human misery is a result of love having gone wrong and when it does go wrong it is often supplanted with power. In a previous section I discussed the problem of shame and guilt. I see them as a symptom of a malignant relationship between love and power. Let us look at this more closely. First of all, the parent has complete power over the child. In fact the parent is in position of absolute power, having total fate control over the child. The parents, through their very activity have conceived and brought the child into being. In essence, parents are gods. What does the child in his/her complete dependence on the parent need most? The child needs to have parents who exercise their power with love. When they do not, shame, abuse or neglect is often the result. This is where the failure to love begins.

Power without love is *daimonic*. If we fail to come to terms with the forces unleashed by the perversion of love and power we will have exactly what we are getting now in our society: the deterioration of communmity and an increase of violence. I define the term *daimonic* as any natural function which has the power to take over the whole person. Sex and Eros, anger and rage, and the craving for power are examples. The *daimonic* can be either creative or destructive and is normally both. The ***daimonic*** is the urge in every being to ***affirm itself, assert itself, perpetuate*** and ***increase itself.*** The ***daimonic*** becomes evil when it usurps the total self without regard to the integration of that self, or to the unique forms and desires of others and their need for integration. This seems to be also a fairly adequate definition for the failure to love. We fail to love when we fail to respect the integration of the other, disregard his/her uniqueness and do not validate his/her desires and need for wholeness.

The failure to achieve a healthy integration of power and love results in a variety of disorders which lead to life long problems. Problems which I have been discussing throughout this essay: ways that power untempered by love functions to disturb and distort the ***self-esteem venture.***

This venture of self-esteem begins in what Erik Erikson calls the earliest and most undifferentiated "sense of identity":

> I would suggest that it arises out of the encounter of maternal person and small infant, an encounter which is one of mutual trustworthiness and mutual recognition. This, in all its infantile simplicity, is the first experience of what in later reoccurrences in love and admiration can only be called a sense of ***"hallowed presence,"*** the need for which remains basic in man. Its absence or impairment can dangerously limit the capacity to feel ***"identical"*** when adolescent growth makes it incumbent on the person to abandon his childhood and to trust adulthood and, with it, ***the search for self-chosen loves and incentives.*** (Identity Youth and Crisis, p. 105)

Erikson pushes very strongly his notion that identity formation is based on the initial encounter which is the basis of attachment and cornerstone of the human personality. This cannot be emphasized too much: love and power have a single root. That root is ***trust.*** This powerful factor, Erikson suggests is what gives us confidence to "abandon" childhood and "trust" adulthood in the search for self-chosen loves and incentives. In other words, in order for us to proceed with our adult *identity venture* we must have meaningful attachments (love) and self-chosen incentives (power). Again Erikson emphasizes the importance of these early experiences for the foundational sense of identity.

> It must be said, however, that the amount of trust derived from earliest infantile experience does not seem to depend on absolute quantities of food or demonstrations of love, but rather on the quality of the maternal relationship. Mothers create a sense of trust in their children by that kind of administration which in its quality combines sensitive care of the baby's individual needs and a firm sense of personal trustworthiness within the *trusted framework of their community's life style.* This forms the very basis in the child for a component of the sense of identity which will later combine a sense of being "all right" of being oneself, and of *becoming what other people trust one will become.* (Identity, Youth and Crisis, p. 103)

We see three very critical dimensions of identity: loving attachment, community lifestyle, and trust. These form both the structure and foundation of adult identity. We see one final and very intriguing dimension also stemming from this all pervasive and important phase: religious faith. How so?

> As we overcome our universal amnesia for the frightening aspects of childhood, we may well also acknowledge gratefully the fact that, in principle, the glory of childhood also survives in adult life. Trust, then becomes the capacity for faith--a vital need for which man must find some *institutional confirmation.* When religion loses its actual power of presence, then, it would seem, an age must find other forms of joint reverence for life which *derive vitality from a shared world image*...The shortest formulation of the identity gain of earliest childhood may well be: I am what I hope and have and give. (Identity, Youth and Crisis, p.114)

Religious faith, hope, community, love and power, crucial ingredients of identity, all stem from the common root of trust. Does this place too much emphasis upon the earliest of human experiences? No, I do not believe so. From my clinical experience I have found that we must acknowledge the primacy and power of the early years. Some would say, in terms of human development, this condemns us to despair if our early years were not optimal in providing us with love and trust. Erikson's contribution, however, balances our understanding. I think he helps us understand the residual themes that have their origins in the earliest and most formative moments which still persist into adulthood. These early encounters with those into whom we were entrusted by fate set the stage for the unfolding of rest of the drama. We cannot love without trust. Without trust we cannot move onto the next stage which is separation. Without trust we fail to establish the embryonic launching pad for our autonomy. Without trust, a growing sense of mastery and competence and our own trustworthiness will not develop.

When trust, faith and hope are shattered early in life, the effects on subsequent phases of development can be devastating. This, in fact, may be where the manifestations of perverted love begin. It seems that if love and faith are not possible then we will opt for whatever is possible. Some find their way by means of power. As Henry Kissinger so eloquently stated, "power is the ultimate aphrodisiac". Others may spend their lives in perpetual "mourning" for that lost sense of "hallowed presence". The variations on this theme are endless. Our goal here is not to catalog all of the permutations but rather to pursue the relationship between love and its failures and how they might be reconciled in authentic adult identity.

Parents who bring children into the world and love them without exercising any parental power do a disservice. Love without power is weak. In order for us to function as adults we must come to grips with the dimension of power and love. In order for society to function as I originally suggested, i.e., in a humane manner, it must also integrate love and power; for at a societal level power without love is injustice, and love without power is anarchy. How do we go about integrating these two sides of the coin? What fundamental changes need to be made in society as well as the family? Let us look at the problem by examining some of our more popular myths which reveal our communal lifestyle and support popular or conventional identity.

> Do your own thing!
> If it feels good, do it!
> Follow your heart!

I think a lot about these slogans, perhaps because I hear people using them so frequently. When I hear them, I always find a sense of irony. I have done my own thing. I have done things which felt good and they led me to make a wreck of my life. Do we really need to be encouraged to follow our heart? After all, what have we been doing? Looking for ecstasy--that certain feeling which comes from instantly gratifying our needs, is the fast track to destruction. Compulsion is a manifestation of a diabolical conflict between the pleasure principle (love) and doing our duty (power). The should's and ought's of conformity and responsibility line up on one side of the conflict with their unassailable appeal to right and godliness (the embodiment of parental and societal power). On the other side is the Self, seeking instant gratification. Rampant narcissism is anarchy.

These slogans suggest antidotes to a life deadened by boredom and by the emptiness of fast-track consumption. When we are bored with our toys and the latest electronic gadgets, we succumb to the appeal of looking for a high. In our adolescent rejection of authority we self-destruct and take a sort of joy in the ability to thwart those around us who try to control our lives. Erikson calls this "negative identity". This is power not grounded in love. Rollo May frames the process in this way:

> The bottom then drops out of the conjunctive emotions and processes--of which love and will are the two foremost examples. The individual is forced to turn inward; he becomes obsessed with the new form of the problem of identity, namely, Even-if-I-know-who-I-am, I-have-no-significance. I am unable to influence others. The next step is apathy. And the step following that is violence. For no human being can stand the perpetually numbing experience of his own powerlessness. (Love and Will, p.14)

It seems to me, then, that violence, apathy, despair, and a sense of futility are all an outgrowth of the failure to love and reach an accord which leads to authentic identity. Doing your own thing is a failed attempt to feel alive in the moment which perverts and then turns pleasure seeking into an addiction or fetish. The perpetual pursuit of love also leads to perverse consequences as it gets turned into an insatiable hunger. "The *daimonic* is any natural function which has the power to take over the whole person."

As I wrestled with the problem over the years, it finally occurred to me that it is not solvable by going with one side or the other. It is a false dichotomy. The solution is neither to be a perpetual child looking for paradise nor a joyless adult who represses all feelings in order to be pious. Getting out of the trap of compulsion cannot be done by fighting ourselves. It requires a new perspective. As reflected by Peter Shaffer's, play, "Equus", in which Dr. Dysart wrestles with the paucity and emptiness of his drab existence when faced with a young boy who blinded 6 horses in a fit of madness. He is envious of the boy's passion but recognizes that he needs to leap onto a whole new plane of understanding in order to be able to reconcile the two worlds. He recognizes that he, as well as his patient, are in need of a new paradigm.

> Dr. Dysart: You see, I'm lost, what use, I should be asking are questions like these to an overworked psychiatrist in a provincial hospital? They're worse than useless; they are subversive. The thing is, I'm desperate. You see I'm wearing that horse's head myself. That's the feeling. **All reined up in old language and old assumptions**, straining to jump clean-hoofed on to a whole new track of being-I only suspect is there. I can't see it, because my educated, average head is being held at the wrong angle. I can't jump because the bit forbids it, and my own basic force--my horsepower, if you like--is too little. The only thing I know for sure is this: a horse's head is finally unknowable to me. Yet I handle children's heads--which I must presume to be more complicated, at least in the area of my chief concern...In a way, it has nothing to do with this boy. The doubts have been there for years, piling up steadily in this dreary place. It's only the extremity of this case that's made them active. I know that. **The extremity is the point.** (Equus)

For me, the new perspective came as I tried to clear up the wreckage of doing my own thing. I found a new meaning in the credo "Follow your bliss:" Joseph Campbell suggests,"If we follow our bliss, we put ourselves on a whole new track that has been there all the time; the life we ought to lead has been waiting to be discovered."

What is this "life we ought to lead?" I think it has to do with loving ourselves but in a different way. There is a kind of bliss that comes from being true to yourself, by gaining personal mastery, meaning and significance, by living life on your own terms. This is authentic identity: love reconciled with power. Love and power when integrated, create a life that provides a sense of contentment and fulfillment which is difficult to attain in our conventional hero systems. This, of necessity fosters and sustains good feelings about ourselves. It comes by making hard choices, delaying impulses, facing anxiety and working through despair and self-hatred. It is a difficult state to achieve, but it is much more enduring. Again, it is a dialectical process which Rollo May describes:

> **A dynamic dialectical relationship**--I am tempted to call it a balance, but it is not a balance--is a continuous give and take in which one asserts himself, finds an answer in the other, then possibly asserts too far, senses a "no" in the other, backs up but does not give up, shifts the participation to a new form, and finds the way that is adequate for the wholeness of the other. This is the constructive use of the daimonic. It is an assertion of one's own individuality in relation to another person. It always skates on the edge of exploitation of the partner; but without it there is no vital relationship. (Love and Will, p.146)

Following bliss demands that we be ourselves--truthfully and relentlessly. Perhaps this is what was originally meant by the phrase "Do your own thing;" but again, was fetishized: doing our own thing without regard for another's boundaries. If everyone is doing it, we ought to be very suspicious. Finding integrity and living authentically is always a lonely venture. But then, if it were easy, everyone would be in a blissful state all of the time. That's why chemicals are so popular, why getting addicted is so easy and why finding an authentic ultimate concern is so difficult. And why violence and power are pandemic.

Following our bliss, then, is not looking for happiness "out there" or in elusive activities which yield temporary ecstasy. As thrill-seekers, we seem to need ever greater stimulation to get the same result. Surfing the increasingly elusive boundaries of hedonism is power cut off from love of self and others. No, following bliss is more a byproduct of finding a personal center and creating a life from there.

> If it is a journey, it is a journey inward! My own conviction has always been to seek the inner reality, with the belief that the fruits of future values will be able to grow only after they are sown by the values of our history. In this transitional twentieth century, when the full results of our bankruptcy of inner values is brought home to us, I believe it is especially important that we seek the source of love and will. ( May, Love and Will, p. 10)

In this infinite universe, the self is an ever changing horizon. As we approach this horizon we do so by integrating feeling and responsibility. Feeling without responsibility is chaos; likewise, responsibility without feeling is emptiness. And I would add a third factor to this credo: feeling without responsibility and without community or context is anarchy. Following our bliss in this new way comes down to doing our duty to ourselves within a context of love and hope. The great question then becomes, not only "what is my duty to myself?, but also, "what is my duty to others?"

This question can be answered by the principle of love. If in loving we achieve the highest state of being human and in evil we find the antithesis of love then the great imperative is to love and in so doing we fulfill our destiny as human beings. To love we must learn to transcend the seeds of perversity and violence within us as well as the forces in our society which support and extol the perversions of power and injustice which dehumanize and form an incubator for all of our social evils.

The failure to love on a grand scale leads to the holocaust. On a smaller and personal scale it is manifested in our own individual holocaust; our failures to love ourselves and those around us. The hunger for love is a powerful motivational force in the human personality, when it is perverted it is no less powerful. It just becomes demonic. When we fail to establish conditions which foster love, such as trust, acceptance, honesty, and caring then we do not create the opportunity for individuals to experience the sense of hallowed presence that is the basis for self-esteem. This leads to failures in our relationships where our transactions do not become "hallowed events". In loving we create a sacred center where all of our transactions support the sacredness of the person. To the extent that we fail to do this then evil prevails.

**NOTES**

# Meditation

# 1

The images were haunting, relentlessly hammering my emotions. My mind reeled and refused to process the incoming information. I had been peddling mindlessly away on a lifecycle at the gym when I noticed a TV monitor showing a building torn apart by an explosion. It was Oklahoma City and for many Americans it was the beginning of a mesmerizing saga of grief, consternation, inexpressible helplessness and impotent anger. It was also the shattering of a national illusion of safety and serenity.

The past few years have turned into to quite a saga. The O.J melodrama had just been reduced to an incessant, dull background noise to the rest of the perversity that surged into our consciousness. The morning headlines scream: "Two Thousand Refugees Killed In Africa"... "We Mourn the 20th Anniversary of Vietnam"... "Commemorating the 50th Anniversary of Dachau". "A Family Is Massacred In Their Beds". And these are just the main stories, the only one's deemed "worth reading" by jaded editors. The daily litany of drive-by murders and other "routine" violence has ceased to impact psyches grown numb from so much mayhem.

What has all of this to do with self-esteem? Do we trivialize great evil with psychobabble? How do we get our minds to grasp the idea of someone intentionally setting out to inflict as much terror and chaos as possible?

As I have discussed these questions with friends and colleagues in the past few weeks, a few ideas seemed to crystallize. The first is that individuals like Ramirez, Dahmer, McVeigh, Hitler,

Jones and Koresh seem to be guided by a singular hatred. At their core is total lack of empathy for their victims.

Those who kill are damaged at a very early age. This is the critical period when the foundations of self-esteem are forming. Such foundations begin, of course, in the attachment bond with those who safeguard our vulnerability, helplessness and dependency.

Positive self-esteem begins with being loved and esteemed by others. It is basic: love of self and love of others is inseparable. Perversity is rooted in a miscarriage of nurturance. It is a failure at a most basic level. The conditions needed to develop trust, competence, significance and meaning are not available.

What was exposed by Oklahoma City is truly frightening. There is a dark, violent underclass of people who are angry, alienated and vigilant. These psychologically vulnerable individuals are finding each other and are coalescing into groups. To their members, such groups serve an important function. They provide a community where members' needs for association, significance, meaning and identification are met. This normal process turned perverse reinforces the participants' anger. It validates their pain and it provides an ideology, an ideology however malignant, that gives them a reason for being.

Give these angry, alienated people a target and weapons and you have a very dangerous mixture; a time bomb waiting to explode, figuratively and literally. Motivation, opportunity, triggering situations and weapons become the recipe for disaster.

The great danger we are facing now is over-reaction. Incidents like Oklahoma City tend to cause people to react emotionally and governments to want to impose more controls and harsher punishments. Fear, anger and helplessness are powerful emotions. When our safety is threatened, we all become paranoid. I do not personally believe that more guns and laws are the solution.

When violence increases in a community, it is symptomatic of deep seated problems which are very complex. Violence is a symptom of failure at many levels in our life together. It is a failure of family, of ideology and of social institutions. These failures result in many individuals and groups being unable to authentically fulfill themselves by meeting their self-esteem needs.

When normal channels for growth and actualization are frustrated, whether in a 4-year-old in day care, an 18-year-old in high school, or a 25 year old in the army, the results are similar. Anger, frustration and aggression result. If viable solutions to the problem are not offered by those in power, then the problem becomes chronic and potentially malignant.

When power and love split at the root in the human psyche, pathology results. When power and love are bifurcated in society, Oklahoma City is often the result. A society of strangers is potentially a society of enemies. What has always been needed and is now needed even more is compassion, empathy and a view of the stranger as brother. We need a harmonizing ideology to bring us together. But transformation always begins with one individual striving to achieve inner peace. As I create peace within and strive for peace with you, we can make a difference. Love and power, when integrated, form the basis for both self-esteem and community. This reconciles and heals the fractured individual and collective soul.

In the words of Scott Peck, it is only in and through community that the world will be saved. Community is the collective expression of love by individuals which has created a context of hope, meaning and healing.

**NOTES**

# Meditation
# 2

How can I possibly love myself? The anguished question came to me from a young man who was filled with self-loathing, guilt, remorse, and shame. He asked it after I told him the solution to his problem was in learning to love himself. He asked, in a shocked and despairing way, "how can I possibly ever learn to love me?" His question reflects the depths of his self-hatred, his alienation, and just how unlovable he feels. In him, love and power is really dichotomized. He can neither love nor experience power.

If we are to lead any kind of meaningful life with some joy in living we must find a way to restore our self relationship. The key to this reconciliation is in finding a way to accept who we have been, who we are right now and, as a result, who we are becoming. This changes our fundamental self-relationship from one of rejection to love. This is critical because who we are becoming is fully dependent on who we are right now. The past, present and future are linked. In this sense we choose and thus create our destiny. We engage in compulsive reenactments because we have not been able love ourselves and hence keep doing the same thing over and over trying to find a solution. Let's look at this more closely. How does this work?

One of my clients, Cynthia, a 70 year old widow, put it this way, "I am amazed that I have such a dysfunctional relationship with myself." What she was discovering was a basic psychological truth. We relate to ourselves and others on the basis of how we were treated very early in life. In other words we internalized the parental uses of love and power. Self-hatred is a deeply ingrained, persistent, and consistent relationship we have with ourselves; it is a reflection of internalized parental power cut off from love. It is so determining because we internalized parental attitudes, feelings and behaviors at a very critical period in our psychological development. This is reinforced over time and with repeated (practice) experience. You know it is a part of you, if when you fail, you respond with, "I knew it all along." There is a perverse expectation that goes with self-hatred. We hate ourselves, expect nothing but grief from our lives--it's what we deserve, and we expect others to feel the same way. If they don't, then we discount them because "they don't really know us." If they did, they would feel the same way we do. Because this expectation is so fundamental it is where we must start the process of transformation.

Psychological makeovers are very difficult. It isn't like getting a new haircut and wardrobe. We have only one life; to live it hating ourselves is such a waste of the gift of life itself. So much is possible if only we could learn to love ourselves. And as I reflect on this simple truth it occurs to me that I could not have learned how to love myself without a long list of loving people in the past few years who gave me the gift of themselves. That's the miracle of the gift of love: *it truly is the gift that keeps on giving. I learned to love me because someone took the time to teach me how. The solution to "learning to love oneself" begins with the recognition of our emptiness and inability to not only*

***love others but also ourselves.*** And that this inability, failure to love, has perverted our very lives. This recognition must lead to a growing awareness of all the subtle ways that our self-hatred plays itself out in our daily melodrama. But even this recognition is not enough because we must find a way to become proactive in our self-love. My dilemma as I discovered it was that I fundamentally didn't know how because I had never learned how. It is hard to change our behavior when we do not have any "life models". It is difficult to create love in a vacuum. The first thing I learned is that in order to love one must learn to trust and overcome all of the old fear and feelings of shame. Learning to care begins with caring about something. I learned to care by taking care of my life. By caring for me and treating myself with respect I was reclaiming lost territory. My therapist gave me a new framework as well as a new life model. As he cared for me, I internalized his caring and treated myself better. He showed me the way. He taught me that each decision I made could be made in the framework of the rule of love. All I had to do was ask myself at this moment in time, what is the most loving thing to do? The trick is in knowing and then doing it.

# Meditation
# 3

    Ambivalence is a powerful dynamic in relationships. Most of us feel very mixed feelings about the people with whom we are intimate. The greater the intimacy in all probability the greater the ambivalence. Ambivalence is usually thought of as love and hate. But I generally think of it as a composite of a lot of powerful emotions. Usually the key to understanding ambivalence resides in understanding what your personal history has been. The key in all relationships is trust. The degree of trust usually determines our comfort in relationships. Trust equals lack of fear and vice versa. Dealing with ambivalence requires a great deal of awareness because most people react to ambivalence by avoidance or their tried and true ways of coping. Let me illustrate.

    Glenn is a young man with a very complicated history of relationships with women. His mother was very ill when he was very young and he ended up bearing the burden of a great deal of care for her. She was quite dependent on him and he felt very resentful of the burden. This is a classic dependency bind in which the child feels many powerful feelings for the caretaker: love, need, dependency, fear, anger, guilt and helplessness. She died before he could resolves this problem.

    This illustrates the first principle of relationships. Our original relationship with a caretaker becomes the prototype for all future relationships. Bowlby, a British psychiatrist studied the attachment paradigm in infants and found that our attachment style established in infancy persisted into adulthood. So naturally, Glenn has had a long history of unsatisfactory relationships with women. In fact, he keeps repeating his mother scenario with every woman he meets. He begins the relationship in the role of good guy/caretaker with women who are rather dependent and needy. He seduces them with his charm and then gets them into bed which is his primary objective. He keeps asserting to me that he does not want a relationship all he wants to do is to have sex.

So he conquers, and they want some form of relationship and start developing an attachment. He, unconsciously wants one too, but becomes frightened and begins feeling trapped. So he starts to pull away and leave the woman, but then begins to feel guilt for abandoning her. So he stays and then becomes enraged and finally starts looking for another sexual conquest. This is a very clear example of the inability to love. Developmentally, Glenn has not gotten beyond his infantile fixation on his mother. When he goes on his crusades to find the perfect sexual partner he is at least moving up the developmental ladder to adolescence. However, his primary problem is in his inability to sustain a stable, consistent, and loving relationship with anyone, primarily himself, of course.

We are working on a number of issues here. The first area of work is on his dependence, which he denies. "I don't need women for anything but sex". It is frightening for him to think of himself as a little boy with all of the fears and needs of that child who had a mother who was so dependent on him. The first thing I have asked of Glenn is to take responsibility for his behavior. I have asked him merely to be clear and direct with women in telling them what he wants and what they can expect from him. Secondly, I have asked him to negotiate his relationships so that he will learn to deal with a woman's expectation without guilt. This is a huge step for him because of his unconscious belief that he is responsible for the woman's happiness and wellbeing. As he does this he is separating himself from his mother and learning to stand up for his own rights and needs. It is difficult for him to not keep falling into the little boy trap.

His ambivalence is the message that he is getting close to the woman. As he struggles to contain and process the feelings at a conscious level he feels an urge to flee, while simultaneously he also feels fear, guilt and anger. When he moves away he feels lonely and empty. So he moves back and forth in the dance of ambivalence: close, distant, close, etc. At this stage I am not asking him to fight it, merely to observe the process and feel the feelings. In this way he is becoming more independent, self-responsible and self-caring. This is the first stage in learning to be self-responsible. If parents subvert the process then it leaves us to learn it as adults. We, of course also struggle through the ambivalence we feel toward ourselves in the process. Going through ambivalence instead of away from it is what leads to transformation.

# Meditation

## 4

English is a strange language, we have ten different words for anger and only one word for love. I love hot dogs, the Dodgers, my truck, movies, Mozart and my son and daughter. Am I expressing the same sentiment when I say I love each? Clearly loving is one of the most profound of human experiences. Notice that I used it as a verb. the Greek language expresses love with three different words: Philos is brotherly love, Agape is godly love, and Eros is romantic love. These words give a little greater precision to the idea of love but even still, the nuances and subtleties go beyond any language. In fact that is probably why we use poetry and word pictures to point toward this elusive something called love.

Our personal definitions are formed by our own histories and experiences. In fact, how we love is probably the most revealing character trait there is. How we love tells whether we are dependent, possessive, controlling, fearful, angry, defensive, passive, needy, trusting, selfish etc. **Our love style is really a manifestation of our core self and how we relate to the world.**

In my clinical practice I have spent a lot of time trying to help people repair the damage brought about by "love". In fact, I often wonder if all the pain, abuse and horror I have seen over the years hasn't affected my view of the possibilities of love. When I look at my own personal history I have to be very careful to not portray myself as a "love expert". In fact, when I sat down to write this piece I found I had a great deal of resistance.

Some of the resistance was in part that I did not want to write a banal, superficial and maudlin essay that was sickeningly trivial. I couldn't possibly add anything new to the discussion and I did not want to write a harps and roses endorsement of the power of love and encourage everyone to do it because it was wonderful. I also recognize my own deficiencies in this area.

So, rather than write about love, I will leave the word out because it is overly utilized and has too much baggage associated with it. Let's talk about the qualities of relationships which produce whole persons. If what ails us is failed relationships (love), then by definition what ought to heal us would be successful relationships (love). Carl Rogers one of this century's greatest psychologists studied therapeutic relationships and found several qualities which he felt were essential to healing persons.

These qualities have to do with warmth, acceptance, genuineness, presence, empathy and caring. This should come as no surprise to any of us that when these qualities are present humans thrive. And when they are absent and their opposite qualities are active in relationships we see the casualties splattered all over the front pages and in our institutions, not to mention the walking wounded who appear normal until they get close to someone.

Erik Fromm also studied love and decided that it was best characterized by Care, Respect, Responsibility and Knowledge. Again, when humans are treated with respect, are cherished and treated with care and knowledge we do very well. If all of this known and true, what seems to be the problem? What keeps us from actualizing these qualities of love in our relationships?

Why does it take years to repair the damage caused by abuse and failed love? More personally, what keeps me from being the loving and caring person I would like to be? These are the questions we need to ask ourselves as we confront our own woundedness, fear, and destructive defenses. These are the questions arising out of our own experience which if taken seriously can lead to greater awareness and freedom to actualize that love and caring which would heal us, our relationships and the world. For it is in loving that we are healed and restored and it is in loving that we build ourselves into the world and it is in loving that we create the possibility that the next generation will be less wounded.

**NOTES**

# 12

# SPIRITUALITY

There are probably no more volatile or ambiguous words which provoke endless debate and controversy than spirituality, God, higher power and recovery. When you put them all together in one brief essay it becomes even more problematic. The first part of the difficulty is that everyone is an expert with a definite opinion. Secondly, even the greatest of thinkers have written volumes on this topic. And thirdly, our language and use of terms is so imprecise that it naturally leads to misunderstanding. What do you mean when you talk of spirituality and recovery? What do you think I mean when I discuss it? A minister? Your sponsor? A Priest? Is it the same if you are a Catholic? A Baptist? A Unitarian? An atheist? A Jew? And finally, are spirituality and recovery related in any meaningful way to mental health and self-esteem.

I believe answers to these questions come from a number of basic assumptions we all carry around with us. Assumptions we may not even be able to verbalize. The first assumption has to do with our image of God: language and belief about this will in large part determine our idea of what it means to be spiritual. A second major assumption has to do with what our image of being human is all about. Usually this comes from our idea about God. Thirdly, ideas about recovery and addiction also are dependent on what we believe life is all about. Most people do not even think about these kinds of questions very often, yet they carry around ideas about these realities and act on them all the time. I once asked a young man what the purpose of life was. He answered, "to live." Not a very well thought out response, yet it was his philosophy of life. We all have one. Our ideas often reflect our cultural context and traditions.

Fundamentally, ideas about recovery, spirituality, and self-esteem come from your philosophy of life. We all have one even if we haven't thought it out completely or put it into an elegant philosophical statement. Our behavior speaks loudest about our philosophy of life, it is our modus operandi; our M.O.. Our world view orders and determines our response to life. "As a man thinketh in his heart so is he."

With all of this as a preamble, then, let me share a few thoughts on this matter. I believe that the deepest and most profound issues in life are spiritual. And by that I mean all of us, in order to live with any degree of satisfaction, must come to grips with these basic questions. Who am I? What is the meaning of life? Who are you to me? And what does it mean to be fully human? If we wrestle with these questions in an authentic and serious manner we will be living spiritually. Not everyone is spiritual even though the basic issues in life may be spiritual. I am fond of quoting my favorite theologian Paul Tillich on his ideas about God and faith. He states that *faith is the centering act of the human personality in response to his/her Ultimate Concern*. What does this mean in personal terms? It speaks to me in that faith is essential to being human. It is what organizes our lives, gives them shape, direction and meaning and makes hope possible. Faith is the foundation of society which provides the context of hope and meaning that under girds its individual members. It is expressed in that well worn phrase, "In God we trust". To paraphrase St. Augustine, "As we confront the ultimate questions of our existence, the self is born."

Faith for Tillich was always faith in something. His insight for psychology is that we become what we worship; that with which we are ultimately concerned. In other words spirituality becomes our defining act. How does this become operationalized on a psychological level? Very simply. We become what we are attached to, what we care about, what we identify with, become committed to, strive after and passionately pursue (ultimate concern). Check it out in your life. If I value fame, money, achievement and success this will become my destiny. In this sense, destiny is the course of our lives which is the sum total of all our choices. Again, Tillich's wisdom is very instructive in his discussion on idolatry. If that with which we are ultimately concerned is not worthy of our worship (idolatry) it will destroy us. I think this is a good description of addiction.

In other words, if we fail to live spiritually and worship lesser gods we may end up wandering about in the wilderness erecting golden idols. Notice how addiction fits this model. It gives you an initial feeling of ecstasy, you feel like you have found paradise, you become preoccupied with the pursuit, you become dependent on the chemical to help you achieve this worshipful state, it takes on ultimate power over you and you sacrifice your self-esteem, health, family and all your earthly goods on its altar, and finally, you take on all the characteristics of an addict; a worshiper whose entire life revolves around serving that god. The god we serve rewards us and punishes us according to the quality of our devotion.

Addiction is a very demanding God. You cannot have any other gods before it. It seems to me that the implications for this way of looking at things are rather obvious. The first is that if addiction is failed spirituality, then recovery must be based in our idea of what spirituality is. Authentic spirituality, by definition, is to be defined by your relationship to your higher power. What we worship; i.e., strive for, care about, value and are devoted to shapes our very being. If we strive to live honestly, authentically, care about others, live responsibly within a moral structure, and seek to live with a sense of meaning and purpose we will fulfill our greatest potential as human beings. In this model self-esteem is a natural outcome. We will not only feel good about ourselves but others will as well. In the words of Jesus, "Where your treasure is your heart will be also. Seek and you will find."

But what is authentic spirituality? Spirituality is not being religious. *I define spirituality as responding to the deepest questions posed by our existence with our whole heart.* How we do this defines us. Again, Jesus had very little patience for the people who were preoccupied with laws, rules and living by the orders of the religious establishment of his day. I think this can also be said of the other great spiritual figures in history. Collectively their wisdom teaches us, "seek and you will find, open your heart, be at one with life, do not be attached to the things of this world, love one another, forgive and live with compassion, and finally, seek first the kingdom of heaven." These are the great but simple spiritual principles that are the foundations of the well-lived life, and for recovery as well. They are one and the same. When we violate them we experience the natural consequences.

What might be some of the qualities of spirituality? Let us look at the spiritual heroes down through the ages, pick one, anyone. The first quality of spirituality, it seems to me is that of *consciousness*. The great spiritual heroes of the past share this characteristic, they are able to see through the "material" world to the eternal realm. In other words they are able to discern values and principles which sustain and restore both individuals and civilizations to wholeness. They are also very self-aware, their consciousness "elevated" and not preoccupied with their own "ego" concerns. In the recent movie "Seven Years in Tibet" the hero played by Brad Pitt was in a conversation with a Tibetan woman whom he was trying to impress with his accomplishments. She made the penetrating observation, "How interesting, you Westerners are so preoccupied with celebrating ego, while we in the East celebrate the death of ego."

Another remarkable characteristic of spiritual heroes is that of *compassion*. They, because of their elevated consciousness, are able to view themselves and others with compassion. They do not judge, condemn nor reject others for being human. This kind of compassion leads to forgiveness, tolerance and acceptance of themselves and others for who they are at this moment in time.

*Caring* is another quality which separates the spiritual person from others. The ability to love another, to love the enemy requires extraordinary abilities. Jesus once said, "What's the big deal if you love those who treat you well, that's easy, but I say to you love your enemy, love those who persecute you and treat you badly." Gandhi, Mother Teresa, Martin Luther King, Buddha, Schweitzer, Jesus, all are recognized by their extraordinary caring for others.

Another quality of spiritual people is that of *congruence*. They are real, genuine, authentic: their presence and power is visible as they let their personhood come through. They are able to be themselves in a way which transforms others around them. There is great power in this kind of congruence.

*Commitment* is readily apparent when we look at the lives of people who have changed the world. They are passionately committed to a cause and to values which transcend them and are of ultimate importance. This kind of commitment prioritizes their lives, it defines them, and gives their lives purpose and meaning. Without passionate commitment they would not have been able to accomplish their deeds and persevere in the face of the opposition they encountered from those around them. They persevered even in the face of death.

These qualities, Consciousness, Compassion, Caring, Congruence, and Commitment have the singular effect of grounding the individual in a dimension which transcends their present life circumstances. They are able to transcend the limitations of their personal histories, their genes, and they are able to transcend the determining effects of their present circumstances, they are able to transcend the limiting perspectives, myths and values of their culture, they are able to transcend their own narcissistic preoccupations, and they are able to transcend their own limiting sense of who they are: their own identity. There is always a debate about spiritual heroes. Are they more special than the rest of us? Are they somehow different? Are they deities who have become incarnate? I think there is a real danger, at least there is for me, when I see a hero as unlike me. I need a hero whom I can emulate. I find little inspiration in trying to be like a god. I can't approach that level of spirituality. Since they are gods it must be pretty easy to pull off spirituality at a human level. But if these individuals have become extraordinary through their choices, their consciousness, their commitments, their caring and compassion which allows them to pursue some elevated image they have of what it means to be a whole human being, then that inspires me to use them as life models. And I think it is crucial to our own identity who we have as our heroes. I think a great deal can be learned by looking at who a society elevates to hero status. A hero is the embodiment of that culture's highest values. The same may be said of who an individual has as a hero. Who are your heroes, your spiritual models?

**NOTES**

# Meditation

# 1

The mystical traditions have as their core practices solitude, silence and relentless inner contemplation. These practices lead to awakened consciousness and heightened spiritual awareness. Psychology has largely been indifferent to or even hostile to this dimension of human experience. It wasn't until the work of Carl Jung and other psychologists who became interested in Eastern philosophy that any benefit could be found in meditation and other spiritual disciplines. I became introduced to the power of solitude, silence, and relentless self-interrogation in a quite unusual manner in 1975. I was looking for a topic for my doctoral thesis when I became exposed to a different kind of psychotherapy. It was called Intensive Psychotherapy. I decided to use an Intensive Experience as the subject of my dissertation. So I spent three weeks in a house on an island in the Puget Sound near Gig Harbor, Washington. The task was to be alone with no cultural props or distractions for three weeks. I was to use the solitude and silence to become aware of myself. I became aware all right, extremely aware! I became immediately uncomfortable with the solitude. I had never been that alone with nothing to do before. The task was to use my immediate experience as the starting point for my self-explorations. The second task was to keep a journal of my discoveries. Then I would see my therapist for two hours a day for five days and then spend the weekends alone. I have come to regard this experience as a "stop the world" event. It changed the way I interact with myself as well as the way I conduct therapy. I have come to have a high regard for the power of solitude and silence as tools for gaining awareness of oneself. The meditation and journalling I did as a result of that experience led to profound insights and an appreciation of my inner life. It also gave me some very important tools for the process of inner questing.

Let me share just a few of the benefits of silence, solitude and introspection: or as I call it, "stopping your world." The first observation I made was how dependent I was on structure, doing, and achieving. The first thing which happens when most people stop their world is that they feel lost, disoriented and anxious. We don't know what to do. Time feels burdensome and the day feels empty. We live in a world of speed, activity and pressure. We rarely stop and get in touch with our inner selves. This is the second component of solitude and silence, no distractions. We are confronted with ourselves in our aloneness we have no one to rely on or to talk to but ourselves. No drugs, alcohol, books, TV, radio, people, work, hobbies: no distractions. I was just there. I became aware of myself, my feelings, my discomfort, my life, and my personal history. I kept coming up with the question, who am I? How did I come to be so depressed? Why was my marriage so dissatisfying? I realized that I did not know "how to be."

In response to my solitude I developed simple routines such as eating, sleeping, walking and writing. I had no other ways of making myself feel better. I had to develop some inner resources. In order to do this I began connecting to my inner experience. I had been totally out of touch with my feelings to the extent that I often felt dead. This experience brought me back to life. A

I often felt dead. This experience brought me back to life. A lot of the feelings were very painful and difficult to understand. But the process of journaling allowed me to pursue what ever I was feeling and let my inner experience unfold. The images, feelings and memories began to connect and create powerful new insights and self-understanding. This led to acceptance, forgiveness and reconciliation with long lost parts of myself.

The net effect was an evaluation of who I was and some new decisions about the course of my life. I came away from this experience on Fox Island with a new feeling of vitality and self-awareness. The analog to this I think would be the vision quest that individuals have experienced where they go into the wilderness and conquer a wild animal and then return to their tribe as a new person. We have few opportunities in our urban culture to transform our consciousness through silence and solitude. I believe that it is essential to find ways to periodically stop our worlds and reconnect with our inner life. This is the source of vitality, and direction which is essential to a spiritual journey. We live in a noisy, machine-technology driven madhouse society where the individual is ground under the wheels of the pursuit of pleasure and things. It is no wonder that we feel empty, disappointed, and bored. The solutions which we are offered only worsen our spiritual condition. ***Stop your world, get to know yourself, and in the silence and solitude of your inner sanctum you will find your serenity.***

# Meditation

# 2

He is an American Icon. Rich, powerful, arrogant and self-assured. He is in control of his life and has the status and everything money can buy. He wants for nothing, he is insulated from all of the cares of ordinary people whom he disdains. He is also lonely, bored, empty and restless. He has an inner sense of something missing: an itch that he can't scratch. This is the plight of our hero portrayed by an American Icon himself, Michael Douglas, in the movie The Game.

I am fascinated as always by stories about metamorphoses. This is a classic hero story. The hero in this case is a wealthy businessman who does not produce anything, he trades in money. He like all heroes begins his hero journey with a wound. A wound he has not dealt with. Healing the wound is the hero deed. His materialism is not satisfying, his spirit is withering. He unconsciously, perhaps on a whim, allows himself to get involved in a "game" with his brother. This is so often the case, that we unconsciously intuit a need and search for a solution. This search often precipitates a life crisis.

This movie is a wonderful parable about our modern predicament. It shows the emptiness yet seductiveness of the illusions of money, power, and status. It also tells us about the process of spiritual enlightenment. In a similar parable as told by Jesus, a rich man approached him and asked him what he needed to do to be saved. Jesus told him, "give all that you have to the poor and come and follow me." The wisdom points in these stories are several. The first is that we are spiritual beings in search of "salvation". Salvation as always is very personally defined. We are looking for solutions to our spiritual dilemmas and answers to the fundamental questions posed by our existence: death, loneliness, meaning, significance and identity.

A second point of wisdom in the Game is that we are known by our attachments. The hero's identity came from what he cared about most. He was passionately devoted to the accumulation of wealth. We are defined by that which we devote ourselves to. His devotion did not satisfy his spiritual hunger nor did it heal his wound.

A third element of enlightenment, and this is the one I find the most fascinating, wisdom always comes at the point of suffering. The great Eastern truth is that suffering comes from attachment. Change came for Michael Douglas as he began to lose control of his life, Control was his first God. He starts becoming uncertain, fearful, and confused. He doesn't know what is going on. He starts to doubt his senses and his own ability. He becomes frantic, paranoid and can't trust anyone, let alone himself.

The next point of attachment is his arrogance. He doesn't need anyone, he thinks. He feels more and more out of control. The next point of attack is his money. He loses it all. And with it goes everything, control, power, status, and his invincibility. He is now touched by all of the things we mortals deal with on a daily basis. He, now to his great chagrin is riding on a bus with the masses, the unwashed masses. He feels embarrassed, helpless, humiliated and frightened. And it is precisely at this point we all find ourselves in our own hero journey. We must turn inward and find the personal resources to respond to the Game. It is how we respond to adversity which defines us.

Money, status, power, fame, control, and the illusion of immortality, these are the great Icons of our culture for which most of us are giving bits of our souls on a daily basis. Few would give them up voluntarily to pursue simpler and more spiritual pursuits. In this hero drama we see an age old lesson, the path to "salvation", leads through the doorway of suffering. Enlightenment comes through death of ego, surrender, humility, and poverty. In essence, these were our heroe's gods. Ego, power, arrogance, narcissism, and love of money. Enlightenment comes through metamorphosis. Transformation comes not always through conscious choices, but in intuitively responding to an inner voice which tells us what we need in order to feed our spiritual hungers. Spirituality comes in honoring the needs of the spirit and making difficult choices to pursue the heroes path. The game of life often presents us with opportunities for change if we but recognize them. Suffering is the window of opportunity for being less attached to our icons.

# Meditation
# 3

Recovery, fundamentally, when all is said and done comes down to one thing: a decision, a yes or no. At some point we must say yes or no to life, to ourselves and to others. What is involved in this decision? Albert Camus an influential author and philosopher of the middle part of this century once said that the only important philosophical question is whether or not to commit suicide. Framing the problem this way puts everything into perspective. Saying 'yes' or 'no' to life then becomes a religious question or at least it has spiritual implications. What is involved in saying yes or no? Fundamentally at some deep inner level we must come to terms with whether or not we want to live or die. If we choose life we must find a way to affirm that it is worth living, that the game is worth the price of the ticket. I think that at the root of the question is Faith. In order to say 'yes' we must have faith that life is possible and that it will be possible to live with meaning, hope and significance.

Secondly, saying 'yes' involves an affirmation of ourselves and life in spite of all of the factors, forces, events, and happenings which tilt the scale in favor of an ultimate no. Death, suffering, absurdity, insanity, injustice, emptiness, loneliness, our own self-destructive potential, and guilt; the list of reasons for not being is probably endless. Each person can always find reasons to hate life or love life. And those who hate life do it from the position of self-hatred. Faith is required for life, and in my experience the reason most people finally come to for not living is the destruction of faith. The loss of hope and meaning is so corrosive to the human will that very few people persist when faith is lost. In spite of the bumper sticker to the contrary, "I feel much better now that I have given up all hope," hope is essential to saying yes. The bumper sticker is a failed attempt to say yes, it is a cynical defense against the loss of hope. It is a defense against the pain of failed dreams and the disillusionment that comes from shattered expectations.

I was in this place a few years ago when I described my life as a bombed out cathedral in world war II Europe. This has become an important metaphor for me in the ensuing years. I now see that each of us has a sacred center from which we live our lives. If that sacred center is in some way desecrated, or impaired then life becomes very difficult. Probably the most difficult problem I encounter as a therapist is when a person calls me in the middle of the night and is struggling to find a reason to live. I cannot give anyone a reason to live, and finding one in the middle of the night is really difficult. What I try to do is to reinforce the search, since the phone call is a person asking for help. But ultimately we must all find our own reasons to be, some reason to say yes in spite of all of our inclinations to the contrary.

The shattered sacred center must be restored and healed. But that cannot take place until the person says yes, and makes a commitment to the restoration. That takes faith. And, I am not talking about faith as a system of beliefs or creeds. I am talking about something which arises from within which calls forth inner strength and effort to keep on going when perhaps everything in us tells us to stop, to give up and check out. This mysterious something is essential to restoring the cathedral. Out of the ruins and artifacts of our shattered lives we must assemble new structures and beliefs, new ceremonies and rituals which will restore and nurture our spirit.

As I wrestled with my own despair, I realized that one does not conjure up new beliefs out of nothing. Nor does one pull oneself up by the boot straps. It is also not a matter of will power. No, for me the most difficult thing to do was to begin caring again. To let things matter to me, and to risk failure, hurt, and disillusionment again was the most difficult thing to do. But in order to do it I had to say yes. Once I said yes, then the rest was learning to trust and to expose myself to risk again. Trust, faith and caring the pillars of recovery. Oddly enough they are also the pillars of life. In affirming life we affirm ourselves. That takes faith and trust. Caring is the way we rebuild the sacred center of our lives. Caring will bring about the wholeness for which we are searching. It is also through caring that we create a context of hope and meaning which makes the recovery journey possible and bridges the isolation that despair, anger, guilt and cynicism have created. Caring also makes possible healing and restoration of the damaged relationships in our lives. But first we must say yes or no, we can't hedge the bet with a maybe. But we do very often try to dodge the issue by worship of lesser gods.

# Meditation
# 4

Recovery implies two things, the first is a set of ideas about what is wrong with us, and secondly what it means to be recovered. In other words, from what to what? We are living in an age of transition where the old gods, myths, symbols and rituals have lost their power to inspire and empower. This leaves us with a condition of failed heroes and failed hero systems. Without "life models" our recovery is made even more difficult that it might ordinarily be. Nevertheless, we are still faced with a very personal need to live with some semblance of significance, purpose, meaning and identity. That the task is confusing, difficult and often overwhelming does not negate the identity quest, it only makes the journey more compelling. I have been operating with the set of assumptions that the goal of human striving is to be as fully human as possible. The debate, of course, rages about what that means. I believe that it is for lonely individuals to decide in their own inner sanctuary what it means to be human on their own terms. That is each person's heroic.

I personally find great inspiration in the work of Joseph Campbell, he shines the light in the darkness for me. To be human for Campbell, is to achieve the ultimate mystical goal, and that is "To be united with one's god. God would be the ultimate elementary idea of man, and we are all made in the image of God. That is the ultimate archetype of man." To be fully human is to actualize the Image of God. Spirituality is the recognition of that which is sacred and being faithful to that knowledge. Our problem today is what it has been for every generation, it is just that the conditions have changed. **Our hero task is to render the world spiritually significant.** Or phrasing it the other way around, it is nothing if not that of making it possible for men and women to come to full human maturity through the conditions of contemporary life. Notice that I am no longer talking about recovery per se. I am talking about the task of discovering what it means to be fully human and then coming to grips with that.

Why is this so important? Fundamentally what is at stake is our core sense of identity. To be fully human means to come to grips with one's life by seeking answers to the questions posed by it. To live authentically is to discover what nurtures the soul and having the courage to pursue the path which leads to fulfillment. A strong sense of identity leads to living with a personal mission, a sense of purpose and meaning which transcends ego and narcissism. What we are searching for is a way of experiencing the world where we can discover the sacred center of life and participate in it. In this discovery we become at one with the reality which creates, sustains, and informs it. Our problem is that we are cut off from this source, we are alienated from the Image of our Creator and hence have become alienated from ourselves and each other.

The recovery journey is the same as the hero's journey, the task and the hero deed is the same. Enlightenment is an awakening to the spiritual significance of life through cleansing the doors of perception. This fundamental awakening leads to a quest, an inner journey whose goal is reconciliation to oneself, harmonizing one's experience with the very ground of our being and establishment of an authentic community of humans who live in accord with these spiritual principles.

The hero lives in accord with the spiritual model of other heroes, by actualizing and making compassion, caring, authenticity, and community real. The hero is one who is actualizing the image of god in daily life. In this way god is made real and manifest in the world. I close with my favorite quote from Joseph Campbell, something to ponder:

> The modern hero, the modern individual who dares to heed the call and seek the mansion of that presence with whom it is our whole destiny to be atoned, cannot, indeed must not, wait for his community to cast off its slough of pride, fear, rationalized avarice, and sanctified misunderstanding. 'Live,' Nietzsche says, 'as though the day were here.' It is not society that is to guide and save the creative hero, but precisely the reverse. And so every one of us shares the supreme ordeal--carries the cross of the redeemer--not in the bright moments of his tribe's great victories, but in the silences of his personal despair. (The Hero With a Thousand Faces, p. 391)

And it is in this silence of our personal despair that our self is born. That is the mystery of life, that is the mystery of recovery. And in the words of Nietzsche, *Hold fast to the hero in your soul, hold sacred your highest hope!*

## *The End and The Beginning*

# Discoveries

**THE STEPCARE INSTITUTE**

Programs and seminars of interest to individuals, institutions and professionals are offered on a regular basis by the Institute. Training and consultation services are offered in the area of trauma, bereavement, addiction, crisis intervention, stress management and recovery.

If you or your organization would like to discuss programs, consultation, or training Dr. Reece is available to help you design and implement a program to fit your needs.

## Available Educational Materials

| | |
|---|---|
| Trauma Loss & Bereavement | $20.00 |
| Stepcare Recovery Guide, A comprehensive approach to dealing with Substance Abuse . | $35.00 |
| Audio Tape Series--Relaxation, Inner Journey, Self-Esteem | $20.00 |

Significant discounts on bulk purchases for institutions are available, please inquire. You may order by contacting

The STEPCARE INSTITUTE
451 W. Sierra Madre Blvd. Ste. N
Sierra Madre, CA 91024

For more information call **626 355 2407** or **e mail** greecephd@earthlink.net
web page **www.stepcare.org**

If you would like to order educational materials please fill out the form below

Name_____

Title _____ Quantity _____ Price _____
Title _____ Quantity _____ Price _____
Address_____
City _____State _____ ZIP_____
Phone _____ Fax _____
    **Add**    **$5.00 for shipping and handling**
                                                    Total_____

www.ingramcontent.com/pod-product-compliance
Lightning Source LLC
Chambersburg PA
CBHW062006220426
43662CB00010B/1253